Awaken

100 Questions To Expand
Your Mind and Open Your Heart

Joseph M. Bernard, Ph.D.

Copyright © 2012 by Joseph M. Bernard, Ph.D.

All rights reserved worldwide. No part of this publication may be
reproduced or transmitted in any form or by any means, electronic or
mechanical including photocopy, recording, or any information storage
and retrieval system, without written permission from the author.

www.explorelifeblog.com

Dedication

*I dedicated this book to all my clients who have taught me
so much about how to be a good therapist and
how to ask the right questions.*

Table Of Contents

Acknowledgment

I can't thank my wonderful wife enough for designing this book, supporting my writing, providing the initial editing and giving me lots of love. Thanks to my amazing sister Joan, who has a very quiet talent for editing that helped make it much more readable. Additional, thanks to our friend Elizabeth, who took the time to read it and add her helpful ideas to make it even better.

Expanding Minds And Opening Hearts

Introduction

This book of questions is based on a very simple premise. That premise is that if you ask yourself questions you will naturally grow in insight and awareness. With more insight and awareness your mind naturally becomes more expansive and your heart opens in understanding. The more expansive your mind is, the higher your consciousness. And the more open your heart is, the deeper your compassion.

There is a great amount of benefit you can gain from this book and its questions. As you explore the questions, do so with the idea that you can achieve more out of life, live more fully and make a positive difference. Remember the questions here are powerful and may cause significant changes in how you see yourself and the world.

Twenty Benefits You Will Receive From Exploring These Questions

1. You will begin to grow into a bigger story of who you are and what is possible.

2. You will feel more alive and energized.
3. You will become more self-realized as a human being.
4. You will find it easier to choose happiness.
5. You will learn to liberate yourself from self-limits and limiting beliefs.
6. You will express more of the endless capacity of your heart to love.
7. You will open to the wisdom and understanding within you.
8. You will be filled with appreciation for all life offers you.
9. You will have a clearer sense of purpose and a greater passion for life.
10. You will feel hope.
11. You will find your way to inner peace.
12. You will make a bigger difference in what you do.
13. You will have greater clarity about the ways you can be successful.
14. You will bring more light into the world.
15. You will be empowered by the wisdom of your mind and heart.
16. You will be more confident in all your expressions.
17. You will be supportive and encouraging of others.
18. You will learn to do life more effortlessly.
19. You will feel more balance and harmony.
20. You will learn to live each day in the here and now and view life as a wonderful celebration.

This is just a partial list of benefits from a deep exploration into self. The inner journey is the part of you yet unexplored. In taking this inward journey you open your life to such richness of experiences and possibilities.

By exploring these questions you will enhance your life and in the process, change the world. You change and the world changes. By raising your consciousness and compassion, the collective capacity expands. Many see the world filled with chaos and fear. This fear and chaos is the creation of peoples' closed minds and blocked hearts. More consciousness and more compassion will profoundly change the world in a positive direction.

Expect to have fun answering these questions. Why do anything that doesn't have a big dollop of aliveness, passion, and fun in it? As you go through these questions don't forget to have a sense of humor. Taking yourself too seriously can be terminal and having fun is just more enjoyable. This process of inward looking is best done with lots of aliveness and a spaciousness of mind that is accepting of your unique qualities and ways of expressing yourself.

Three Guiding Principles
1. Take all the time you need.
2. Be easy with yourself.
3. Enjoy the journey.

As you explore the questions you may sense the energy that went into the creation of this book. If you tune in, you will be able to feel the vibrations of support and encouragement that comes to those willing to take the journey of self-realization. These vibrations you feel come from the power of your intention and from the energy of the heart of the collective consciousness. Tune in and ride the waves of heart and mindful intention to serve you as a constant support on your journey.

"The hope of this book is to awaken the highest possibility in you as you explore the questions in pursuit of your own higher knowing and truth. The only real truth is what you find within. The only true knowing is beyond the confines of ordinary thought."

The Way To Use This Book

The optimal way to use this book is to get a journal or open a Word document and start exploring the questions. Writing is very helpful because it moves the thoughts from a closed circuit mind dialogue out onto a page where they can be examined. This gives you a way to clarify your thoughts, which is always a good thing.

You can also use these hundred questions as an inner practice for the next 100 days. You read one question each day. Let it stir inside. Then take the time to write down the answers as they start to inform your thinking and touch your heart.

Clarity is what you seek and this kind of expansive clarity is more likely to come from a higher knowing then the word-stream of your thoughts. Your higher knowing is located beyond the ordinary mind in what may be called the Higher Self, intuition, Spirit, the sacred heart, wise mind or by other names. This expansive knowing can be expressed intuitively in the writing as you let it present itself.

The format of the book is to present the questions and invite introspection and contemplation. Then, let the ideas take hold in your heart and vibrate with your higher mind. As you sit with the questions, insights and awareness will come to you. Listening inward with the purpose of new awareness and understanding is the way you grow and deepen as a person.

There may be layers of past programming, old beliefs and stale thinking in the way but those will come to the surface as you explore. Take the old ideas and beliefs and see if they still fit. If they don't, replace them with the new, higher levels of knowing.

How Do You Change A Belief?

Beliefs are a collection of words to which you give meaning, often repeatedly. You can change any belief by being aware that: *first*, you have this belief; *second*, ask if is it working for you — is it true from your present understanding; *third*, do you want to re-examine this belief or change it; and *fourth*, what do you want to replace this belief with?

One of the goals of this exploration is finding your own truth. The truth can only be understood in the now — in the present moment. The truth feels right. It is usually energizing and inspiring, and it can feel calming and peaceful.

The structure of the book is about asking questions that bring insights into who you are and what your life is about. These insights open you up to understanding yourself, the world, and the truth with greater clarity. The result will be more self-acceptance, acceptance of others, and a clearer path of purpose and meaning.

The questions are designed to take you into a much deeper understanding of yourself and your many as yet unexplored capacities. The most rewarding journey of life is the exploration of your soul and higher nature. The

following is a list of what you may discover about yourself
through your inner explorations:

- You will find the voice of your inner wisdom; your
  intuition.
- You will learn how to access your inner purpose.
- You will discover inner abilities you didn't know
  you had.
- You will gain awareness into your unlimited
  potential.
- You will more fully explore and express your
  uniqueness.
- You will touch into the wisdom of your heart and
  feel the depth of your compassion.
- You will be shown how to be free in this lifetime.
- You will develop a relationship with your higher
  nature/spirit/soul.
- You will see the truth of higher consciousness and
  the unity of all living things.
- You will better understand how you can create
  meaningful relationships.
- You will have a deeper understanding of yourself
  in the world and the positive impact you can have.

As you explore these questions, be aware they can
be very intense. You are encouraged to pace yourself in a
way that allows a deep exploration done in the spirit of
compassion for you and for all that may get stirred up.

Going Out Into The World

After the extensive journey inward, the questions in this book move towards: how to have meaningful relationships and how to move out into the world in ways that will enrich you and those you interact with. This part of the journey is where you grow with others. Your shared insights inform how you work together and how you express your purpose in the global community.

The potential of insightful and awakened people getting together to bring about positive changes in the world is exciting. Imagine a day where the light in you interweaves with the light in others and together you create a tapestry of inspired ideas and solutions to the needs and issues on the planet.

"One day the light goes on in enough people and the world takes another step in its conscious evolution and things change forever."

Hints To Help

There will also be a **Hints Section** with each question. These hints will include additional questions and ideas to help spark a deepening of the question process and to encourage more awareness and insights. Sometimes questions may seem obviously clear and other times the mind can get tripped up by words. The hints will help clarify what is being asked and invite a more expansive search into the deeper nature of the question.

The hints can be skipped if you choose to just stay focused on the questions.

One last thought: be gentle and supportive of yourself on this journey and take the time to appreciate and enjoy your new insights.

ARE YOU READY FOR THE JOURNEY?

The first four questions depend on each other to get the full picture of what they are asking. These questions, when explored, will greatly enhance your awareness of who you are.

Now let's begin the questions with the focus turned inward.

PART 1

Finding Your
Own Truth

1

Go inward and ask,

"Who Am I"?

HINT:

This is one of the great spiritual questions. Your answer to this will change as you deepen your awareness but for now explore who you are as fully as you can. It is okay to look ahead; question one and two are closely related. Who is the seer within when you see?

2

Are you your personality, your body,
your thoughts, your emotions?
If not who are you?

HINT:

Your personality, body, thoughts and emotions may be seen
as outer expressions of your higher nature. Many have
sought to answer these first two questions. The truth lies
within a more expanded knowing of what/who exists
beyond your physical and psychological manifestation.

3

Are your thoughts real?
What is the knowing beyond
the ordinary mind?

HINT:

What if your thoughts were nothing more than words to
which you give meaning? If that is true you can always
change what you are thinking to change how you are feeling.
How do you find your truth without thinking? Here are
some suggestions to expand what you may include in
exploring the "knowing beyond the ordinary mind." Some
examples of that may be; wisdom of the heart, mind of
spirit, higher mind, Higher Self, inner voice, intuitive
knowing, Divine wisdom, observing mind and others.

4

What have you learned from the first three questions that will expand how you view yourself?

HINT:

Are you able to be okay with aspects of yourself not yet understood? What can you understand through your intuitive higher mind? Along the way you may discover that you are not what or who you think you are. Is the uncertainty of who you are something you can be okay with?

5

What is the source of your inner knowing and the messages of guidance you can hear inside of you?

HINT:

What is intuition, gut instinct, or the wisdom of your heart?
In what ways do you receive your inner guidance —as
feelings, inner voice, pictures or other ways of knowing?
Could these messages be the voice of your soul?

You are off to a great start with the insights you have gained from these first five deeply-probing questions. You will continue to feel more acquainted with yourself as you go through these questions. The first five were complicated and they will be re-examined later as you acquire more insight. Remember that these questions are about finding your own truth and about being a person who understands who you are and more of what is possible within. Just the asking brings insight into your true nature.

6

What do you know about your heart and its capacity to love and be compassionate?

HINT:

The heart center is more of what this question is about. Are you limited or unlimited in how much love you can give? How does self-love affect your capacity to love others? A heart can be open or closed. When your heart closes to someone it affects your ability to be open to others.

7

How have you been able to step away from the chaos of your own thoughts?

HINT:

Do you understand what it means to step back from your thoughts? How do you access an observer/witness self?*
Meditation, mindfulness, yoga, centered prayer and other practices can assist the stepping back process. Imagine being above yourself and being able to watch what is going on in a loving, accepting and peaceful way.

The observer/witness self is able to watch you and your thoughts free of judging. This quality of impartiality, of watching without being critical is a very powerful ally in understanding yourself and realizing what is possible within you.

8

How do you find inner peace? What is the importance of self-love and self acceptance?

HINT:

How can you be confident and at peace if you are critical or disapproving of yourself? What if a positive self-esteem was the key to a better life. How could you approve of yourself? Life will be more relaxed and joyous if you are accepting of who you are. People who are not able to love themselves have difficulty loving others.

9

How do you deal with problems in your life? Do you seek solutions or spend most of your time reacting to what you think is wrong?

HINT:

Do you have inner solution consciousness or outer solution consciousness? Do you search within for solutions or go looking for others to make things happen?

10

In what ways does your thinking shape the experiences of your life?

HINT:

How does a negative stream of blame and complaining make you feel? How does a positive stream of hope and understanding make you feel? How would a quiet and peaceful mind shape your experience of living? A busy, chaotic mind has difficulty being at peace with itself.

Excellent work!!! You have come this far and made it through the first 10 questions. I send you lots of encouragement and a warm surge of energy from the collective heart of compassion. So far you may have more questions than answers, new insights into who you are and excitement about this exploration. Those questions and their answers are important. Be sure and write them down. Later you will know how to call upon your higher nature to give you the answers that seem important.

Are you having fun exploring? If not stand up and turn on some music that makes you want to move. Let your body express itself or write a poem about something you thought was crazy but now see differently.

What ideas in the first 10 questions have gotten you excited about life? Where are you thinking you want to lighten up, to make some healthier choices to move in a more positive direction?

Take a break and only move to question #11 when you are relaxed and ready — when your dancing shoes have cooled off.

Ideas to change your energy:

Read something that inspires you.

Watch a funny video.

Get up and go for a walk.

Pet your dog or cat.

Call a friend you have been missing.

Do something creative.

Make some cookies.

Do some exercise.

Hug your partner.

Take a nap.

Visualize something you want to do.

Plan a trip.

Do some stretching.

Go have a glass of water or a snack.

11

What do you know about your judging mind? Are you generally more understanding and accepting of self and others, or are you more judging and critical?

HINT:

What would those around you say about your understanding or your judging way of being in the world? Are you hard on yourself? How does that work to make you happy? We humans can be judging machines. How would you go about breaking that habit?

12

What do you know about the feelings that you experience? Do you feel your feelings or push them away? Are you able to acknowledge and accept your emotions?

HINT:

Feelings are caused by our thoughts. Feelings are just the energy of our thoughts. How do you let the energy of emotions flow through you? If you get caught in the intensity of an emotion, you can take a few deep breaths, relax and let go of any negative energy. Emotions, if watched, soon change to something else on their own.

13

What feelings have you been ignoring which causes you to numb out in your life?

HINT:

Suppressed feelings become tension in the body. How do you release pent up emotions? Where you sense numbness, there could be unexpressed emotions stored there. Exercise can be an energetic way to release emotions; so can expressing them through journaling or processing them with others.

14

If happiness is a choice, what choices are you making to be happy and what choices are you making that keep you from being happy?

HINT:

President Lincoln said, "People are as happy as they choose to be." Many experts on mental health and personal well-being say similar things about choosing happiness. Happiness begins inside and is not dependent on the world around you. If you look to others and situations as the source of your happiness, you will be disappointed often. Each day you can *choose* to be happy. Wouldn't that be nice?

15

If appreciation helps create happiness, what do you need to appreciate today to be happy?

HINT:

Appreciation and gratitude are sure formulas for happiness because they are experienced inside of you. Allowing appreciation to be felt lifts you up and creates a feeling of happiness. This choosing to focus on appreciation is to choose to be happy. Being fully present also naturally gives you access to joy, love, hope and inner peace — all part of what inner happiness is.

BONUS HINT:

Sometimes things get stuck and our mind gets knocked off track. You then may need to do something out of the ordinary to get the train rolling in the right direction. Things like going for a drive, watching a fun movie, calling up a supportive friend can do much to help you feel better.

The exploration of these first 15 questions has invited new self-awareness. Were you aware that happiness was just a choice away? If you don't believe that idea, choose to be happy today and see how your mind gets in the way of that choice. Each time you notice a mental obstruction, remake the choice to be happy. After a few days of re-choosing to be happy, it gets easier and life will be more fun.

16

What beliefs did you learn growing up that need to be revised? How do they limit you and your life today?

HINTS:

Like most, you probably learned not to believe in yourself; that you are not deserving of the life you want; that you are not smart enough and many other false and limiting beliefs. You may never have taken the time to closely examine these beliefs. It is time to do that as you take this journey guided by these questions. There are many beliefs that need to be looked at to see if they are your truth at *this* point in your life.

BONUS HINT:

Other examples of false ideas might include thoughts like; desire is wrong, money is bad, fear is necessary, sin is a reality, or the color of a person's skin or their beliefs makes them unacceptable. Watch the mind and see what beliefs come up throughout your day. Be especially watchful of ideology or dogma. You will be surprised if you are mindful of your own inner conversation. You will discover that many of your thoughts are based on false beliefs. If you leave no belief unexamined then you are moving toward an authentic life.

17

How come you have stopped questioning what needs to be questioned?

HINT:

Your mind is busy running its program of thoughts that go unquestioned. In a busy life it is easy to become overwhelmed and not take the time to really search for your own truths. It may seem simpler to ignore what seems too complicated or just do what you have been told. Questions, however, can help reclaim what you may have lost by taking an easier path. When you question your own thoughts, you have the opportunity to free yourself from how you hold yourself back.

18

What matters most to you?
How well are you living
what matters to you?

HINT:

If you say your family matters most but you have little time
for them, then the importance of that value needs to change.
How you spend your time is a reflection of what matters.
Values are important to prioritize. They serve as a guide to
how to live your life.

Values to Explore

Make a list of your top ten values and prioritize them in order of highest to lowest of importance. Use the top three values to guide your life. Listed below are some values to consider. Feel free to add your own.

Love	Control	Hope
Family	Spiritual	Respect
Pride	Peace	Money
Growth	Career	Being Right
Power	Honesty	Friendship
Creativity	Fitness	Compassion
Perfection	Giving	Security
Fame	Patience	Looking Good
Home	Calmness	Intimacy
Awareness	Kindness	Approval
Party	Touch	Mastery
Loyalty	Doing	Acceptance
Being	Caution	Curiosity
Ambition	Fun	Cleverness
Faith	Trust	Imagination
Simplicity	Beauty	Serving Others
Abundance	Solitude	Empowerment
Devotion	Dignity	Getting Even
Energetic	Confidence	Risk-taking
Genuine	Frankness	Mind Power

How do you wake up when
you know you have been
sleep-walking through life?

HINT:

If you are asleep, you don't know what is going on inside of
you. You may not even know your own thoughts or how you
feel. This can make life seem scary and unpredictable. Ask
your heart, ask your higher nature, ask the wisdom of your
body. Listen for your intuitive guidance and be present
throughout your day to what is going on inside.

20

What of your past is affecting and limiting your life today? What do you need to release so you can live your life in the present?

HINT:

Whom, including yourself, do you need to forgive? What unfinished business are you hanging onto or are unwilling to move on from? Are there past relationships, job frustrations, negativity towards parents and more lingering inside? It's time to stop beating yourself up about what *was* and move on. Letting go is very liberating.

Wow! You are doing well to be here reading this. These past twenty questions have invited you to look inward. How does that feel? What new insights have you more excited about yourself and the possibilities for your life?

Now that 20 questions have been explored, how are you going to be nice to yourself for your efforts? How about giving yourself a reward — like a day doing your favorite activities? Can you allow yourself to have fun? If not, don't go any further in this book.

Instead ask yourself these two additional questions.

1. What keeps you from having fun?
2. Are you ready to make the changes needed to cut loose, to be less serious, and to go out and enjoy life as fully as you can?

Wait to move forward until you know you are open to having fun in your life. Remember, being too serious is dangerous to your health and makes you a boring person.

21

How do you explore, learn
and grow in your life? What
new ways of growth have you
been exploring lately?

HINT:

If you are not growing, you are not feeling okay about
yourself. Growth is being engaged in the world with your
mind, your body, your emotions and your spirit. Are you
having meaningful conversations? Do you read thought
provoking or insightful books? Do you explore inner
practices of any kind? Many report that the inner journey
of self-exploration is the most fascinating part of life.

What do you know about your inner critic? What are you willing to do to change your inner dialogue toward being more supportive and encouraging?

HINT:

The inner dialogue is the conversation that goes on in your head almost non-stop. You have an inner critic as part of that dialogue. Have you ever heard the critic at work in your own mind? Often if you listen to the voice of the critic, it sounds like a parent or someone else that was unkind in the way they tried to control you as a child.

23

How does seeking the approval of others get in the way of your life?

HINT:

Approval-seeking happens because of self-doubt/low self-esteem. The only true approval happens within. Not from those around you. This need for the approval of others can ruin your peace of mind and make you ignore your own truth.

24

Why is it healthy to acknowledge and accept your feelings?

HINT:

If you deny how you feel, you feel less okay about yourself. Feelings tell you when you are on course or off course. If you acknowledge how you feel, soon another feeling replaces it. Unexpressed emotions may adversely affect your health.

25

Why is taking responsibility for yourself essential for your well-being?

HINT:

Blaming others and situations makes you feel powerless. Taking your power back is as simple as taking responsibility for your life. *You* are the creator of your life experience.

Your thoughtful answers of the last five questions help you to feel more positive about yourself and your experience of life. You have within yourself an unlimited source of wisdom and light. You are meant to more fully realizing who you are and who you are capable of becoming. As you keep stretching your mind and the view of yourself, you open even more to being the empowered creator of your life.

26

Why is it important to do self-care of the mind, the body, the emotions and the spirit?

HINT:

Taking care of your mind, your heart, your body and your spirit is about bringing out the best in you. If your mind is open and peaceful, your body is well cared for, your emotions healthily expressed, and you are in touch with your spirit then you are in charge of your life. Each day do something that nourishes each of these four aspects.

27

How come life's lessons are so important?

HINT:

Life lessons help you grow and become more aware. If you continually ignore important life lessons, they may come to you again with more force (imagine a relationship ending because you didn't listen.) Lessons learned enrich who you are.

28

What if there is no limit to how much you can love? What ways will you open more to loving?

HINT:

There is no limit to the heart's capacity to love. Love can be in the form of compassion, kindness and caring. Loving takes you from a mundane life to one filled with the joy of heart.

What makes you feel most alive?
What gives your life meaning?

HINT:

If you are feeling alive and energized that is a good sign that you are right where you need to be. Having meaning in your life is something that has heart, feels purposeful and touches your soul. Life without meaning seems bogged down and lacks aliveness.

30

How do you find your own truth and why is that important?

HINT:

Can someone else tell you what *your* truth is? Is dogma or ideology from someone else ever your personal truth? An open mind is necessary in the search for truth. When you live according to your own truth, you can find peace of mind.

BONUS HINT:

Self-searching and self-examination are powerful and sometimes challenging activities. If your energy is up and flowing then you are resonating with your own truths. If you find yourself tired out by these questions then stop and tune inwards. It is time to go looking for where you are stuck or holding back. This is about freeing yourself to what is possible.

When stuff comes up that feels too much, it is often best to go talk with a friend who is a good supportive listener. If that isn't enough find a counselor who listens well and is fully present. That is usually what is needed if healing the past is called for. Letting go is a very important part of this process.

31

How do you get in your own way?

HINT:

Are you hard on yourself? Do you have old ideas about yourself and the world that are holding you back? You know if you are in your way because you keep getting the same results; those which you have been trying to change for quite some time. Old stuck places sometimes take some digging around to uproot what is in your way

32

What limiting ideas of who you are need to be changed?

HINT:

Your self-concept can be tainted by responses to your childhood, by trauma in your life, by thoughts from your past and other negating experiences. These old influences need to be removed through awareness and a more in-depth journey toward your soul.

33

Why is it important to increase your sense of self-worth?

HINT:

How much you value yourself shapes how much you value others. If you don't value what you want or what you need, then you may have difficulty supporting others needs and wants. All ideas that you lack worth or value are totally false. In this moment if you can feel your heart, be open in your mind, and be in-touch with your spirit, you will know clearly that you are an amazing human being.

34

What walls need to be
taken down inside of you so
that you can come out into the
world more authentically?

HINT:

Life sometimes is complicated, disappointing and hurtful.
What walls have you constructed in your mind or heart that
keeps you safe from past experiences? Are you willing to risk
taking those walls down? If not now, when?

35

If blaming makes your feel
powerless and angry, then
what would empower you
and make you feel hopeful?

HINT:

Blaming and complaining are crap magnets. The more you
complain and blame, the more you have to blame and
complain about. Self-empowerment is essential and it
happens by seeking solutions, by taking action, by living
with purpose and by putting love into what you do.

Five more are done. How are you feeling? Just a reminder to be easy on yourself and remember you are doing this over a matter of weeks or months so you have lots of time to let these questions percolate. If you find yourself pushing through these questions to get them done, step back and take a breath, go for walks, have fun with friends and talk about what you are exploring and learning.

I also highly encourage you to use meditation or mindfulness to support this inward journey. These practices will enrich your life in many positive ways. They are the bedrock from which many of my questions arise. The benefits of these inner supportive practices are numerous and provide a space for answers and clarity to come.

Mindfulness is like meditation brought out into the world. In mindful practice you are fully present to what is going on inside your mind as you go about living your life. An example would be you paying attention to your thoughts and feelings while you are doing a project at work. In that process of tuning in you may hear a note of resentment in your voice. That awareness of resentment then invites further exploration. With mindful exploration comes the possibility of setting yourself free from emotional entanglements or at least notice them when they appear.

36

What keeps you from fully
loving yourself? From whom did
you learn you were unlovable?

HINT:

This second question is about those who shaped your sense
of self. Recently I heard a mother of a very upset child say,
"Can I trade my child for your nice bag?" I am sure the
mother was tired, but what kind of message would that
child receive from hearing that? Most of us heard messages
like that growing up. You can release these old limitations by
becoming aware of them and having the intention of letting
them go. This process of awareness can assist in the healing
of whatever wounds may have been caused by the unkindness
of peoples' words and actions.

37

How do you let your thoughts and emotions trip you up?

HINT:

Thoughts are just words you give meaning to, emotions are the energy created by your thoughts. Both your thoughts and the emotions they create can get in your way. Think of the last time you had a thought that sent you into feeling worry. That worry grows larger the more you feed it. Mindfulness is a great friend in helping to notice your thoughts and what feelings they create. When you hear how you think, you can see how that affects your ways of being in the world.

38

How do you block the emotions
you feel uncomfortable with?
How does that limit your
experience of other feelings?

HINT:

Blocked emotions turn into tension in the body. Block any
emotions and the other emotions are affected. If for
example, you are afraid of your anger, your may sit on it —
hoping you won't blow up. Eventually you blow because you
have been building a charge of anger inside. Sitting tightly
on your anger would also block your ability to love.

39

What thoughts do you need to change to have peace of mind?

HINT:

The mind can be very disturbing. Recently I passed a guy on the beach who was mumbling and swearing under his breath. It was on a beautiful day in a beautiful place. He was experiencing his ego driven mind, too upset to appreciate the moment. Do you spend more time being present and pleasant, or elsewhere and upset?

40

How would acknowledging and accepting all your emotions affect how you feel about yourself?

HINT:

You might notice that many of these questions inquire about your emotions. The most powerful thing to do with your feelings is to tune in, feel them, and accept them. Every time you acknowledge and accept you how you feel, it validates you as a person. All feelings come and go naturally unless you try to hang onto them with your obsessing mind.

You have explored 40 questions. To succeed this far is a very powerful affirmation of who you are and your commitment to be even more of what is possible within you.

Congratulations!

You are an exceptional human being. Please take the time to appreciate you and your efforts.

You may notice that some of the questions are similar and yes, that is intentional. Asking several questions about the same concept can bring different angles of insight and awareness.

41

How do you shrink the voice of the inner critic?

HINT:

This is another question about the critic and it asks you to go exploring more deeply. The inner critic is not your friend. It does not make you a better person and it is only good at beating you up. The inner critic needs to be shrunk down to a distant whimper so the voices of the past no longer haunt you. To do this, notice as often as possible when it speaks and imagine turning the volume down like you would on a television or music device. You could even imagine zapping the critic with your mute button.

How to shrink the inner critic:

+ Be aware of it.

+ Catch it when it speaks inside.

+ Listen to who it reminds you of.

+ Imagine turning the volume down on it.

+ Replace critic with words of self-love.

+ Change your inner dialogue to be supportive.

+ Appreciate who you are.

+ Be okay with all your feelings.

+ Make positive statements of support and encouragement.

+ Have compassion for who you are.

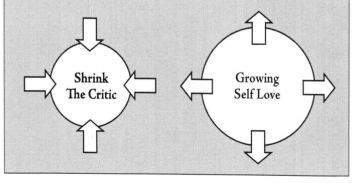

42

Why is self-appreciation healthy for you? How do you acknowledge and appreciate the things you do well?

HINT:

Self-appreciation is the opposite of the inner critic. Every day you do many things you can acknowledge and appreciate. Appreciation brings you genuine happiness. Take a few minutes right now to make a list of what you appreciate about yourself and look at it when you need a boost.

43

In what ways do you take care
of yourself to promote
your well-being?

HINT:

Your well-being is the key to a life of health. Consider this:
if you eat right, keep fit, get the rest you need, stretch often,
quiet your mind, feel your feelings, listen deeply to what you
need, then you are bringing more healing and health into
your life.

44

When you feel out of balance,
how do you bring balance
back into your life?

HINT:

What is balance for you? How does it feel? When you lose
balance, things feel "off" and you usually sense it is time to
make some changes. If, for example, you are spending lots of
time reading and researching, you may be neglecting the
needs of your body, your heart or the connection with your
soul. If you are meditating 10 hours a day then other things
are probably not being attended to. Balance is the play
between the demands of life and your needs.

45

Is personal freedom important to
you? In what ways do you limit
your freedom? How could
you free yourself up?

HINT:

Freedom may or may not be a driving force for you. Do you
want to be free? What would freedom be for you? You are
the one that places limits on yourself or the one who sets
you free. Freedom means you are able to be, explore and
express all of you because you have gotten out of your way.
The mind is too often a jailer.

The last five questions are important ones in the journey of setting yourself free. The significance of balance and freedom are different for each of us. Some can go way out there in their lives and find a balanced way of living that feels very alive. Others find freedom inside in the way they express themselves through their art. Life is totally unique to each of us. If you find people to share your uniqueness with and they enjoy the journey with you, that is a real blessing.

Take some time in the next few days and appreciate those who support your inner journey — your exploration of who you are. They are important and often add strength to your determination. Everyone appreciates being appreciated.

What have you learned or are you learning about the importance of patience? How can you become more patient?

HINT:

We live in a very fast paced world where we expect everything *now*. Where do you need to be more patient; in traffic, with those around you, in line at the grocery store? Can you practice slowing down enough that you can relax into the moment? Breathing with awareness is a great way to slow down and add a touch of patience to whatever you are doing.

BONUS HINT:

Breathing with awareness is simply watching the cycle of the breath; the inhale and the exhale, and the point of transition from the inhale to the exhale, and from the exhale to the inhale. As you notice this breath flowing in, pause. Then notice the breath flowing back out, then pause. Repeat this process of breath flowing in, pause and the breath flowing out, pause. Noticing the endless cycle of the breath is very calming and relaxing. This practice also brings you into the present where joy, love, peace and hope reside.

Most people are good at listing their flaws. What are your personal strengths?

HINT:

How about making a list of 10 things you do well. If this is an effort, then it is time for a big dose of self-love and appreciation. If you were asked to list what you do poorly, would that be an easier list for you? Build on what you do well and find ways to grow into things you want to do better.

48

What human potential in you is waiting to be explored?

HINT:

You have an unlimited potential. What inside is calling you to be expressed? I recently turned 60 and gave up my idea of running in the Olympics. But that in no way limits other options for me. I could organize a Senior Olympics and run in that. Or become a great endurance runner and win my age division. How about writing a best selling novel about someone's journey to becoming an Olympic athlete?

BONUS HINT:

What are some potentials you can explore: learn new languages, write poetry, be an inventor, explore and create methods for self-healing, take up golf, learn a martial art, broaden your consciousness through meditation, become a famous pie maker, join a toastmasters group and give talks, find new ways to build meaningful communities on the Web, write songs that will inspire people, or make movies that change the world. There is an endless list of potentials in you waiting to be expressed.

49

How do you express yourself creatively? If not yet, how will you find ways to be creative?

HINT:

Creativity is part of who we are. Exploring creativity makes you feel more alive. You could be a creative genius as a parent, as an innovator in communications, as a collage maker, as one who expresses love, as a writer of short fiction, or millions of other creative expressions. Like the expression of your potential in the previous question, the ways to be creative are endless. What calls you to be creative?

50

In what new ways are you exploring and experimenting with your life?

HINT:

If you view life as a grand experiment then you give yourself lots of leeway because there are no failures, just feedback about what is working and what is not yet working. Imagine you take this day and do an experiment on love. In that experiment, you keep your heart open wherever you go and whatever you do. You just notice how people respond to you. If you don't notice a difference than maybe your heart already shines brightly.

You are now half way through and you have done a super job exploring the first 50 questions. These questions may be more than many seriously ask themselves in a lifetime. This speaks highly of you and your depth of commitment to awaken.

So from here on take the time to go deeper into what feels right to you. Deeper means you use silence to open to what more you can understand about who you are and how to make the best of the crazy world we live in.

Also these questions can have a feeling of lightening you up. I once heard that "angels can fly because they take themselves so lightly." All the heavy stuff isn't heavy if you can step back and watch, and not get caught up in the drama. More on that as you continue.

51

How have you been expressing your uniqueness and what new ways are you thinking about trying?

HINT:

You are one-of-a-kind. There never will be another you. If you settle for a half-hearted version of you, we all miss out. Where are you holding back expressing who you are? What ways do you need to move out of your comfort zone? You being yourself fully will without a doubt leave the world a better place.

52

What ways are you having fun and enjoying life? What do you need to do less of — and more of?

HINT:

If you are having fun you can thank yourself. If you are not having fun and enjoying your life, look in the mirror and see who is getting in your way. Life is about having fun and being who you are as fully as possible. Sometimes people learn things growing up that limit their fun. The goal as an adult is to unlearn what is not enjoyable and to learn new ways of experiencing joy.

53

Emotional well-being is important. What emotions do you need to get better at expressing and releasing?

HINT:

This question invites you to move toward more awareness and healthy expression. Unexpressed emotions can eat away at you, make you feel uptight, and block your heart. What emotions tangle you up the most? How can you learn to release them in healthy ways? One of the simplest methods for releasing challenging emotions is to acknowledge what you are feeling. This acknowledgement of your emotions changes how you feel almost immediately because to acknowledge is to be respectful of yourself.

54

The present is all you have to create the life you want. How often do you get stuck in obsessing about the past or worrying about the future? How do you plan to stay in the now?

HINT:

The now is where all the action is. If you are stuck on what happened before now, or what will happen tomorrow, then you will be too busy to notice and partake in what the moment has to offer.

55

How can you live more fully in the present moment?

HINT:

Living in the present is the only place to be if you want to be successful. *Now* is rich with possibilities and hope. The optimal mind is in the *here and now* with positive thinking and the power of enthusiasm. There are many practices to help you be present. Mindfulness and meditation are two that help you learn to be in the now. If you take the time to tune inward and breathe into the moment, the now is where you will find yourself.

Another five question milestone. You must really be gaining confidence from your dedication. This exploration has nothing to do with inflating the ego, and everything to do with being a more fully realized human being. You are taking the steps right now to move your life forward. Nice job. Keep it up and spread love and light along the way.

Today take a step away from the ordinary. Try driving home a different way, walking through an area you have always wanted to explore, or go shopping in a store you have always wanted to wander through. Are you having fun yet?

56

Does worry ever change anything in a positive way? What would be a better thing to do than worry?

HINT:

Worry never works. If it did I would worry about not having enough money in my bank account and then watch the funds increase in proportion to how much I worried. Wouldn't that be nice? All worry does is get you stuck. Instead focus on positive actions to take.

57

Everyone is imperfect. How do you deal with your imperfections? How do you improve on who you are?

HINT:

If there is always room to improve does that keep you motivated? Perfection is something to strive for in an effortless-effort kind of way. Doing your best in this moment is a great start. These questions are a self-study program on personal improvement.

58

Who would you like to become?

HINT:

This is a very open ended question and one which may take some time to answer. Relax your thoughts, take a deep breath, and let your imagination go wandering into all the possibilities that come to you. When you get clear about this question, then you will become that person and the world will be a much brighter because of it.

59

Now, for a way-out-there question.

If you were granted three wishes from which all of humanity would benefit, what would those three wishes be?

HINT:

This question is about thinking with everyone in mind; thinking with a global mind; and thinking as if you were responsible in some way for your fellow human beings. Are you ready for that big of a job? Your heart is.

60

There is a knowing beyond your mind. What is that knowing?

HINT:

The answer to this question is not something the rational mind will find easy to come up with. Go inward. Communicate with the higher knowing in you. This could be your soul, spirit or Higher Self. See if you can rise above the noise of your endless thoughts. This illustration is about three states of mind; the isolated state of ego-mind, the more expansive knowing of higher mind, and the great wisdom of infinite mind.

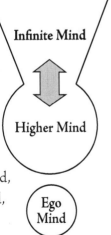

Infinite Mind

Higher Mind

Ego Mind

Sixty questions have now been completed. How are you handling these recent questions that are inviting you into a deeper concentration? Hang in there. The light gets brighter and the insights can totally alter the way you view the world. This first question may seem like a high hurdle to cross, but the backstretch is in sight.

Today, who you think you are will begin to change because you are seeing things in a more revealing light. If you keep this up, soon you will be fluttering like a butterfly that has just been transformed or like a running back that sees a big opening and runs through it towards the goal posts. You are on the way and things will only get more interesting.

These next several questions will take a slightly different direction. In this new direction you will be asked to make contact with your higher nature to assist you in your responses. Don't worry. The answers will come naturally after all the exploring you have been doing.

PART 2

Seeking Your
Higher Nature

61

What part of you is infinite and eternal? How do you make contact with what is and always will be?

HINT:

Beyond ordinary thoughts and body needs, there is a part of you that was there before you came here to this life. That part of you will continue on after you pass. Imagine you are traveling through time; who/what is this traveler? If you sit quietly, can you make contact with the part of you that is eternal?

62

What does it mean that you are
a spiritual being having a human
experience — not a human being
having a spiritual experience?

HINT:

What is your true nature? Spend time with this question,
letting deeper guidance help you discover your true nature.

63

What is your Higher Self?
What is your Soul?
What is your Spirit?

HINT:

Are these separate aspects of being human, or are they
different names for the same thing? Are you acquainted with
any of these expanded human aspects? To find the answer
to these questions, you must find out who you are beyond
what your ordinary mind would describe you as. In the
stillness of the now, beyond the noise of the mind, there is a
much wiser and compassionate light.

64

What do you know about the power of silence in your life?

HINT:

If you don't know about the power of silence, it is time to go exploring. As a way to answer this, go some place where you will not be disturbed. Tune inward. Lots of things will get stirred up. Can you sit through the initial storm of the reactive mind and find the peace inside? Once in that place of inner peace, open yourself to what guidance is patiently waiting for you to listen. Meditation and mindfulness practice are golden doorways into the silence.

65

What is the collective consciousness?
How would you connect with
this shared consciousness?

HINT:

There is a knowing that represents all human knowing and
it resides some place beyond our ordinary view of the world.
Tapping into it may be as simple as becoming still and
opening the mind and heart to guidance. Try plugging into
this consciousness by imaging a cord from your mind being
connected into the vastness of knowing and the limitless
energy of compassion available in the highest consciousness
on the planet.

Have the last seven questions stimulated your higher mind? I hope you are enjoying the direction these questions are taking you. As you expand in your awareness of self, your understanding and exploration expands as well. This is where the journey gets even more interesting. When you are willing to courageously go exploring into the infinite, you will find so much to be excited about and grateful for.

66

What is the oneness we all share?
What is unity consciousness?

HINT:

This idea of oneness is really amazing when explored. What if there was nothing separating you from every living being except the limits of your thinking? Imagine the place in you that is in constant realization of how we are all connected. In this place of unity, feel what it does to your heart.

67

If spreading light and love was your purpose, how would you live your life?

HINT:

Since spreading light and love is my purpose, I love this question. In many ways it seems we all share that purpose. We certainly all have the capacity: to awaken, to love, to raise our consciousness and to develop compassion for each other.

68

In what form did you exist
before this lifetime and what will
continue after your body dies?

HINT:

Most religions have an idea of an afterlife but more as a
destination of either glory or punishment. What if there is
no heaven or hell but an evolution of your soul? What is
your sense of what of you existed before this life and what
will continue after? Is there such a thing as reincarnation?
Do you live this life hoping for something better after death
or do you live life to the fullest today?

69

What part of you is using these
questions to learn and grow?

HINT:

What is the part of you that expands in wisdom? Is it your
mind, heart or soul? Maybe life is about awakening to
what you already know. Does learning and growing bring
you closer to the realization of your highest nature or the
Source?

70

What is your higher nature?
How do you communicate with it?

HINT:

What is the difference between *self* and *Higher Self*? There is in you a connection to the Source of all creation. That is what people call a spirit or soul. Where does the part of you that is spirit connect to the part of you that is human? How do you know when your higher nature is communicating with you?

Now that 70 questions are part of who you are, how do you feel about yourself? How does feeling more expanding shape how you experience the world?

Your exploration has been exceptional. I trust fully, if you have come this far, that it is of real benefit to you. These questions do not have right answers but they do have your answers; answers that matter to you. Your exploration of truth is so important for you and for the rest of the world. As you become more enlightened, your light enriches all your interactions. This inner light invites the light in others to shine. The more the light in all of us turns on, the more things change for the better across the planet.

Exploring these questions expand consciousness in you and those around you. At some point the light in all of us becomes so bright that the darkness in the world gives way to the highest realization of our compassion and consciousness.

How have you taken the
information that your thoughts
are not real from early in these
questions and used that to change
your experience of life?

HINT:

Your thoughts are simply words you give meaning to.
Nothing more. If you have thoughts that are getting in
your way or limiting you, then you can change those
thoughts today. Thoughts shape your experience of life. If
your thoughts are negative, life can be stressful. If they are
positive, life can be wonderful. Change any thoughts in this
moment that are limiting you.

72

Where do you find hope inside?

HINT:

The source of hope for you may be different than for others. Hope naturally arises in the now — in the present moment. Hope does not exist in the future. You can feel hope about tomorrow, but that has to be in the here and now. Is hope a thought? Is hope a feeling connected to the heart?

73

What knowing guidance
in your heart do you need
to pay attention to?

HINT:

The heart is intuitive. The heart has the intelligence of emotions and has unique ways of sensing. It is a power source with many cells capable of cognitive processes. It has the ability to spread healing. An open heart is infinite in its capacity to love, to heal, and to know.

Your intuition is a powerful guiding force. How are you doing paying attention to intuition and following its guidance?

HINT:

Intuition is an inner knowing message system that communicates with you through feelings, pictures, words, sensations and through synchronicity. If you listen inward, you will find there is always guidance available to you. If you follow the intuitive guidance, good things happen. If you ignore these inner messages, especially the repeated ones, suffering often happens. To say you don't know what to do is not true.

75

How do you nurture the growth of your mind and expand your thoughts?

HINT:

Your incredible mind needs to grow or it can slip into obsessing about what it can't control. It can be run by fear if it doesn't have new ideas to explore and integrate. The mind benefits greatly from meditation and mindfulness practices because of the richness of insight and awareness they offer.

The 75ᵗʰ question is a jump off point where you can be like Indiana Jones in one of his movies where he was faced with the unknown. He could take the risk of crossing the invisible bridge or hold back in fear. A risk-taking mind is open to adventure and growth. A fear-driven mind closes down. The mind can be the great liberator or the maximum security jailer. If you are truly interested in personal freedom, which getting this far in this book would clearly indicate you are, then your mind needs to be trained as a valuable asset or it will play the saboteur to what you want to create in your life.

Mindfulness, meditation, yoga, tai chi, chi kung, contemplative prayer, out-of-body-experiences and many other inner practices all can be wonderful ways to train the mind to support your liberation. In most communities there are opportunities to find classes that teach inner practices. If you don't have opportunities for classes there are many books to read, CD's and DVD's available. In the back of this book is a list of resources that offer materials for inner development.

76

If you were able to quiet the judging mind and you didn't feel the need to judge everything as either good or bad, how would that change your life?

HINT:

Our minds can be judging machines. Everything we judge as good or bad is from the ego-mind. What if there was no good or bad but acceptance, compassion, kindness, or seeking understanding? There are those who seem dark minded but they are wounded souls who have lost the way to their own heart. Those lost souls represent a very small number when compared to the amazing human possibilities in all of us. Even those that spread fear with their words only do so because they have lost touch with the intelligence of their heart.

77

What does it mean to be self-realized?

HINT:

You have your own ways of being realized and those ways change as you awaken to even more of what is possible. Take a minute here to sit with the idea that you are unlimited. That means you can do anything, be anybody, go anywhere. It is all up to you. Your self-realization is a blessing to the rest of us on the planet. Make a plan for how you want to be more realized. Move into action and enrich yourself and the world.

78

What kind of healing do you need physically, emotionally, mentally, and spiritually to be whole?

HINT:

What wounds do you have from the past? Have you mended your experiences of a broken heart? What trauma resides in you and your body that needs release? How do you get in the way of your healing? Your imperfections are no dark mark on who you are, but simply parts of you that need to be reclaimed. The hurts from the past are in the past. Today you are infinite in what you can be.

How do you recognize the force of the ego-mind in your life? How does the ego-mind limit you? If you wanted to replace the ego mind from directing your life what part of you would you call on?

HINT:

I realize this is a series of complicated question. The Ego-Mind is about protecting you from worries. It is run by its many fears. This mind seeks to control all it can. The Ego Mind is only doing what it thinks is right but it is overly protective and too controlling. The exciting news is that there is a Wise Mind in you also. The doorway to Wise Mind is in the quiet of the moment.

80

What do you know about your Wise Mind? How can you let it guide your life?

HINT:

Your Higher Nature is the location of the Wise Mind (that is if these ideas of what exists had any physical location). The concepts of Higher Mind/Wise Mind are ideas to be explored and experienced. The ways of the Ego-Mind can often be easily noticed. Next time you are afraid, see how the Ego-Mind is present. The Wise Mind/Higher Mind can go unnoticed if you don't listen inward. This inner knowing is beyond the thoughts of your ordinary mind.

You have completed 80 questions. That is incredible. You deserve a pat on the back and a big hug from the Universe. Can you feel the energy of the inner support you have acquired along the way? I send encouragement from my heart to you and your efforts.

Now there are twenty questions to go. Soon the tone will change again to help bring your newly found understandings out into the world in constructive ways. These deepening questions are such an important part of the journey of life if you want to explore your potential and be all you can be. The next few questions will keep things going in the same deepening way so enjoy them.

Now turn on the cruise control so you can make it the rest of the way as easily as possible. Enjoy the wealth of the moment and the accumulation of what you have learned along the way.

81

How do you quiet your mind? How do you become more mindful?

HINT:

This takes practice and there are many different methods of meditation and mindfulness. Two practices that can be very helpful are breathing with awareness and expanding the heart through loving-kindness. These practices will make a positive difference in your life. There are references at the end of the book that will have information on where to find out more about these practices.

BONUS HINT:

My favorite practice is walking meditation. In this practice I pick a park, trail, beach or some comfortable area to walk through. I begin to watch my breath and walk in a relaxed manner. I find later in the evening or early in the morning to be nice because it tends to be quiet. As I walk I appreciate my breath, the beauty around me and the quiet of the moment. Soon the walk finds its own pace and the outside world drops into the background of just being full present.

82

What ways do you express your purpose? What is your inner purpose? What is your purpose in the world?

HINT:

A purpose-guided life is what most people are looking for especially as you get older and feel the need for more meaning. You have a specific purpose(s) that is unique to you. No one else will ever express that purpose in the way you can. Your purpose may evolve over a lifetime. Living your purpose makes you feel fully alive.

83

Being positive is not any more right than being negative. But being positive is a much more enjoyable way of going through life. How could you be more positive?

HINT:

A positive frame of mind works better. A negative frame of mind can make life harsh. Optimism helps create the kind of life that is enjoyable and happy, and it brightens much of what is experienced. Your thoughts shape whether you experience life from a positive or negative viewpoint. If you want to have a better life, start by making sure your thoughts are positive.

84

How would your life change if you changed the way you viewed yourself and the world?

HINT:

Your sense of self and the world totally shapes how you experience it. As a positive frame of mind fills your life with more light so too will a life that focuses on giving and helping others. Also, a life that is about exploring your spiritual nature or about expressing your unique gifts more fully will feel very enriching. If you play the blame and complain game, your life will not be much fun and the world may seem hopelessly entangled. If you look with light in your eyes and a warm heart, each day will create the hope of what is possible.

Are you open to connecting with others? How well do you do that? Or are you too protected? How do you plan to become more open?

HINT:

It is not unusual that people have life experiences that cause them to choose to close their heart down. Have you had such experiences? How have you worked through that or are you still in the process of healing? An open heart is key and an open mind is also important. A judging and fearful mind pushes people away and keeps you protected.

That is 85 questions you have explored with gusto. This next section heads down the path of building relationships. If you can figure out how to be okay with yourself and open to building relationships with others, then the journey is going to be filled with many wonderful possibilities.

Can you feel the end is near? Are you ready to integrate your new insights into how you relate to others? Now you get to go through the next set of questions and see what interesting things come up.

I remember a famous meditation teacher talking about spending several years in a meditation retreat and when he returned home, his past struggles with relationships were still there. He had done all this inner work and it took just a brief interaction with others to knock him off center. Everyone learns from his or her relationships.

Many would say life is all about building relationship with those you love, those you work with, those you serve, those in your community and those fellow travelers on this tiny wet rock out in the middle of an endless universe.

PART 3

Building Relationships

86

What ways do you allow intimacy into your life?

HINT:

If there is no intimacy in your life, you are most likely shut down in some ways. Intimacy can be a best friend who you can talk about anything with. It can be the way you connect to your brothers and sisters, children or grandchildren. If you keep your distance or have trouble working through difficulties, then you may be more guarded than you realize. Being guarded is the work of the Ego-Mind. That can be changed by bringing your focus to a place of trust in the wisdom of your heart and the endless capacity of your soul.

How are you able to feel
compassion for others?
How does that allow you to
get close to another person?

HINT:

Compassion is being open to understanding another. What
opens you to compassion? How does having compassion for
your own struggles affect your ability to have compassion
for others?

BONUS HINT:

Here is a loving-kindness practice. As you sit or lay in awareness of your heart let it spread the light of caring through your body. Feel the peace of that caring. Then imagine that light of your heart flowing towards someone you love. Feel how it feels to bring another into your heart. Then your caring heart flows toward all those you love. When you have filled them all with your loving-kindness, now spread your loving-kindness to people you work with and interact with. Feel how uplifting that can feel. Then let your heart's warmth fill your community. Now let it spread to cover the planet. Feel what it feels like to have compassion for everyone and everything on the planet. This is the kind of capacity you have for love.

88

How would you spread more loving-kindness in the world? How would your relationships be if they were based on loving-kindness?

HINT:

Loving-kindness is loving through the kindness of how you interact with those around you. Everyone deserves to be treated with loving-kindness — especially you. Even people who can be difficult do much better when they are treated with loving-kindness. It almost always feels good to help others who are stuck by giving them big doses of loving-kindness.

89

In what ways are we all alike? How does that help open you to others?

HINT:

To know that you, me, and everyone else are similar is to allow others closer — to open to the idea of trusting each other. Being open begins with trust of self. Imagine that we all share similar desires and hopes. In reality there is much more common ground than differences between all of us.

90

Sometimes you can get stuck.
How do you ask for help when
you need it? Where do you
turn for support?

HINT:

Are you able to ask for help or do you have to do it on your
own? Do you allow yourself to connect with people so you
can feel okay to ask them for what you need? Can you be
open and vulnerable and still ask for help?

Now the countdown 10, 9, 8 ... and you will be fully renewed. Tony Robbins says if you work for 1% improvement per day, in 100 days you will be 100% improved. This is the same for asking yourself these questions. Each question is worth 1% improvement and after these 100 questions you are 100% an improved version of yourself. Exciting, isn't it?

91

How do you create meaningful relationships with others?

HINT:

Meaningful relationships are so enriching to your life. They are an important part of your life as a social being. If you find yourself without any meaningful relationships, a good place to start is to build one with yourself. Once you feel okay with *you,* you can find others who are all right with themselves. People who feel good about who they are can have many meaningful relationships.

92

What is compassionate listening and why is that an essential part of building meaningful relationships?

HINT:

Which kind of friend do you appreciate the most: one who is better at giving advice or one who listens with compassion? Is it advice you are looking for when you are struggling or is it to be heard, supported and understood? A compassionate listener listens with an open heart and mind and is fully present to what is being said. Most listening is done impatiently, as we wait for our turn to talk.

93

How do you empower the people you are in a relationship with?

HINT:

Relationships are at their strongest when they bring out the best in each other. The qualities of patience, acceptance, support, appreciation and encouragement seem important in relationships.

94

How do you push people away?
How would you change that?

HINT:

Some people are really good at pushing people away. Can you think of someone like that? It may seem safer to keep people distant and your heart protected. Inviting people into your life feels so much better.

95

What people do you look up to?
How have they influenced
who you are?

HINT:

The models in our life tell us a lot about who we are. If you look up to people who are rough and tough then that makes you want to be rough and tough and be with people like that. If you appreciate people who live by the highest values then that will be the kind of person you want to be and the kind of people you like to get close to.

The last five questions are going to shift once more toward an even larger perspective. This is the last bend on a very long and winding road. Can you now see the finish line?

Beyond relationships, how do you connect to the bigger world? These questions are big picture ones and when explored can have a profound affect on the world. This is where the rubber meets the road, if you are an advocate for social change. This is about how you take your ever expanding self out into the world to benefit all.

You have been doing excellent work. You have the right to appreciate how dedicated you have been to this process. Now let these next 5 questions be the frosting on the cake of a celebration called an extraordinary exploration.

96

How can you express more compassion in your life and for the people around you?

HINT:

If you want to promote real change, the essential component is an open compassionate heart. Love literally can be the solution to all the world's problems. If people decided to change the world all they would have to do is bring together the compassionate energy of their hearts. Love has the capacity to set us all free.

97

Why is there so much anger and fear in the world? How do you release your anger and resolve your fear?

HINT:

The base emotion of all negativity is fear. People are afraid of what they can't control. There are many things in the world that seem out of control. The place to begin is to resolve the fear within. Fear cannot exist in the now when there is an open heart. Try it for yourself if you want to experiment. The now is free of fear because it is not about controlling the future or replaying the past. In the now the heart reigns; joy, love and peace arise naturally.

98

How come your individual expression is so important for you and humanity?

HINT:

You being you as fully as possible is a positive and powerful force in the world. The world today is full of people living by other people's ideas and beliefs. Many are so bogged down in survival that they live in fear for tomorrow. This all can change by you and the rest of us moving into our greatness — into expressing our genius. That full expression of you will be a beacon to guide the rest of us.

Where are your purpose and passion being expressed for the good of the world? What causes matter most to you and what are you willing to commit to doing to move those causes forward?

HINT:

These questions are wordier because there is a lot to them. You and only you can live your purpose. You're the note that will make the symphony of life complete. You are the missing piece to the whole puzzle of how we thrive in the midst of such change. Whatever cause is calling you, it is time to take everything you've got and get involved.

In the silence of this moment answer this:

What is the reason you are here at this time in history and how can you best serve humanity?

HINT:

What are you here to give? How can you give in meaningful ways? Listening inward will show you what to do if you want to know. Maybe you feel too busy? Most of us do feel overwhelmed but that can't get in the way because waiting for more time tomorrow may never come. These are amazing times. You are here to do something that is so needed by all of us. Please do what you can do today and every day.

It has been awesome traveling with you. Your light will be enlightening the rest of us. You have the energy to help recharge and uplift the world. There never has been a more awake you and the awareness and insights you have gained have joined the collective consciousness and made us all much better for it.

I appreciate your efforts and your light. Peace, love and happiness to you in this moment and as your journey continues.

If you want to get in touch with me, have me come and give a presentation or lead a retreat or workshop, I would love to. I can be reached at josephteach@hotmail.com.

I write most days at my blog, www.explorelifeblog.com, if you want to continue exploring your life.

Resources

The following are some of my favorite books because they inspired me to ask questions about my own life:

1. Power of Now - *Eckhart Tolle*
2. A New Earth - *Eckhart Tolle*
3. Being Peace - *Thich Nhat Hahn*
4. Old Path White Clouds - *Thich Nhat Hahn*
5. The Miracle of Mindfulness - *Thich Nhat Hahn*
6. Way Of The Peaceful Warrior - *Dan Millman*
7. The Law Of Spirit - *Dan Millman*
8. The Alchemist - *Paulo Coelho*
9. You Can Heal Your Life - *Louise Hay*
10. The Joy Diet - *Martha Beck*
11. Be Here Now - *Ram Dass*
12. Book of Secrets - *Osho*
13. Illusions - *Richard Bach*
14. Hypnotizing Maria - *Richard Bach*
15. Siddhartha - *Herman Hesse*
16. The Power of Intention - *Wayne Dyer*

17. The Seven Spiritual Laws of Success - *Deepak Chopra*

18. Conversations With God - *Neal Donald Walsch*

19. Wherever You Go There You Are - *Jon Kabat Zinn*

20. The Autobiography of a Yogi - *Yogananda*

21. A Path With Heart - *Jack Cornfield*

22. A Return To Love - *Mariannne Williams*

23. The Power of the Subconscious Mind - *Joseph Murphy*

24. The Law Of Attraction - *Ester Hicks/Abraham*

25. How God Changes Your Brain - *Andrew Newberg and Mark R. Waldman*

26. Adventures Beyond The Body - *William Buhlman*

27. The Untethered Soul - *Michael Singer*

28. Just One Thing - *Rick Hanson, Ph.D*

Note: *Most of these authors have a number of other books worth reading.*

Other places for inspiration:

In addition to reading, there are many resources on the Internet. You can find more inspiration on sites such as:

www.soundtrue.com

www.ted.com

www.shambhala.com

About The Author

Several years ago, I had a moment of insight that woke me up to what was possible. I decided then that I wanted to live life as a fun adventure with unlimited passion. I knew I needed to follow the guidance of my heart and that my mind needed to expand to tap into my extraordinary life.

As a therapist for 35 years, I fine-tuned my skills of compassionate listening and asking questions that provoke and encourage insight and awareness. I have assisted many in finding their way towards a meaningful and rewarding life.

On the journey I chose psychology and the wisdom traditions of the East to help others. I continue to be active in: living life to the fullest, keeping fit and enjoying competitive sports, exploring higher states of consciousness, practicing meditation, mindfulness and yoga, expressing creativity as an artist, writer and blogger, and working for social issues including peace and the well-being of the planet.

I welcome opportunities to teach, give presentations, lead workshops and retreats, and coach those who are seeking to be more successful through mindfulness, awareness, creativity and leaving their past limits behind.

21920668R00084

Made in the USA
Lexington, KY
04 April 2013

Dennis Koranek

From Lightning to the Light

A Novel

Pleasant W*rd
A Division of WINEPRESS PUBLISHING

© 2007 by Dennis Koranek. All rights reserved.

Pleasant Word (a division of WinePress Publishing, PO Box 428, Enumclaw, WA 98022) functions only as book publisher. As such, the ultimate design, content, editorial accuracy, and views expressed or implied in this work are those of the author.

No part of this publication may be reproduced, stored in a retrieval system or transmitted in any way by any means— electronic, mechanical, photocopy, recording or otherwise— without the prior permission of the copyright holder, except as provided by USA copyright law.

Unless otherwise noted, all Scriptures are taken from the Holy Bible, New International Version, Copyright © 1973, 1978, 1984 by the International Bible Society. Used by permission of Zondervan Publishing House. The "NIV" and "New International Version" trademarks are registered in the United States Patent and Trademark Office by International Bible Society.

Scripture references marked KJV are taken from the King James Version of the Bible.

Scripture references marked NASB are taken from the New American Standard Bible, © 1960, 1963, 1968, 1971, 1972, 1973, 1975, 1977 by The Lockman Foundation. Used by permission.

ISBN 13: 978-1-4141-0893-3
ISBN 10: 1-4141-0893-1
Library of Congress Catalog Card Number: 2006910116

To the glory of God.

Table of Contents

PART 3: RETURN TO THE LIGHT

Preface

There are no such things as coincidences in life. God is in control of everything. He takes care of the sparrows and knows how many hairs are on our heads. Things that happen in our lives that we question may have happened the way they did because God has planned events to carry out a specific purpose. We wonder why people are sick or die at times that may be premature. Sometimes we find out the answer and sometimes we don't. The Lord may bring people into our lives at certain times for a single purpose and then we are left wondering why. We may or may not ever find out.

Some of the events of this book may appear to be disjointed or loosely coupled but are specifically meant that way. What the reader will not see until the end of the book is that the Lord knows of events that will happen in the future and has planned for them far in advance. Thus, a chain of events takes place that could only have been orchestrated by God. Characters are used for their intended purposes and then the reader is left wondering what happened to them. Some characters and situations are developed to show specific traits of the character but are not developed further since their purposes had been served. Most chapters were developed to not leave the reader hanging.

Dennis Koranek

Acknowledgments

There are many people who supported me in the writing of this book. Though I'll never cover them all, here are some that had the most impact:

- My lovely wife Linda, who tolerated me during this entire process.
- My sons Micah and Simeon, who read the story as it was being written to see if there were any major blunders.
- My daughter Kristina, who began the editing process.
- My coworker Ken King, who provided ideas on time travel and the idea of having a female superhero.
- My computer class student Sandy Childress, who provided some review and needed editing.

Part 1

Doctor Lightning

The Storm

"Hurry up, honey," said Sara. "You'll be late for your own graduation. This ceremony may be just a formality, but we'll have to boogie big-time to get there on time. Glad you're not going to be an OB/GYN, or you'd never get paid for your work."

Matthew and Sara had only been married for a couple of weeks. Matthew had just finished interning, and this was the final ceremony before he could open a real doctor's office in town. Sara had graduated as a registered nurse several years before, but the couple had needed to wait until Matthew finished interning before they could open their own family practice. As they both liked kids, they decided to go into practice together. Eventually, they would have kids of their own, but for now they decided to work on establishing their business and helping other people's children and families.

Matthew was a procrastinator and tended to run late. He also tended to be forgetful. Sara was a caring person and made a wonderful nurse. She was very detail-oriented and all the patients at the hospital were happy to have her as their attendant. She loved her husband very much and had not minded supporting Matthew through medical school. Although they shared a house for a long time before marriage, it did have three bedrooms and two bathrooms, and they had agreed to not intrude on each other's space before they had wed.

"I'm sorry, Hon," said Matthew. "I just had to finish watching this DVD."

Matthew was a cartoon addict. He considered watching cartoons an escape from reality, and he found it served to ease his tensions—for a while at least. In a twisted sort of way, this passion would soon be a factor in how his life would change.

"We should have left by now. There's supposed to be a horrific storm, and the likelihood that we'll even find a parking space is getting slimmer all the time."

"OK, I'm about set." Matthew said this as he put on his suit jacket and headed for the door. Sara gave him one of those looks people give when someone has forgotten something important but hasn't yet realized it.

"Aren't you forgetting something?" Sara looked down at Matthew's feet, which made him look down as well.

"Oops! This will only take a second." He quickly slipped his shoes on and headed for the front door.

"Is it my imagination, or are those socks different colors?"

"Nobody will be able to tell with these long pants on."

Sara looked toward the ceiling and just shook her head. They made it out the door and headed for the car. Matthew went ahead and opened the car door for her.

"Allow me," he said as he opened the door.

"Why, thank you, my dear knight in shining armor," said Sara. She giggled as she slid into the passenger's seat of the car. She looked quite lovely in her formal blue gown, blue high heels, and white shawl. A pearl necklace enhanced her long elegant neck. Her curly blonde hair draped over her bare shoulders.

Matthew shut Sara's door and went around to the other side, sliding into the driver's seat. As he turned the ignition key to start the car, thunder rumbled.

"Hope we beat the storm," said Sara.

"We'll beat it. Have I ever let you down?"

"No, but there's always a first time."

The sound of thunder grew louder as they drove up Monkey's Head Road. This road was particularly treacherous in bad weather, as it was very curvy and there were many trees that hung over it. On a normal day this would have been a very pleasant drive, especially if you were riding in a sports car.

Matthew was used to the car. Although it wasn't new, or even a sports car, it had front wheel drive and handled decently in bad weather. Yet the rain was coming down in sheets and visibility was low even with the wipers set on high.

"I don't like this," said Sara. There was a tone of concern in her voice.

"That makes two of us! Personally, I would prefer to get to the ceremony in one piece and a little late than not get there at all."

Just then, there was a flash of lightning immediately followed by deafening thunder. Out of the corner of her eye, Sara saw a huge tree on the right about one hundred feet away begin to fall across the road. Matthew, who was watching the road in front of him, didn't notice the tree start to come down until about a second later. At thirty miles per hour one second equals forty-four feet, so by the time the tree hit the ground, there was only about thirty feet between the car and the main trunk of the tree.

The only words Sara could get out of her mouth were, "Watch out!"

With no real time to avoid the tree, Matthew swerved and attempted to slow down as best he could. The torrential rain simply made the problem worse. The car went broadside into the tree's branches, and Sara's side took the damage. A large, long limb crashed through the side window, hitting Sara in the head. She was killed instantly. The limb narrowly missed Matthew as the car came to a full stop. It all happened so quickly that neither of them could have done anything to prevent the accident.

Matthew turned to Sara, and what he saw instantly put him in shock. Her head was only partially attached to her body, and blood was spraying out all over the tree limb and the rest of the car. Rain was pouring through the window and mixing with the blood. Matthew knew that she was dead and that there was nothing he could do. He burst into tears, losing track of time.

When he came back to reality, the storm was in full force and even seemed to have intensified. Matthew's mind whirled. He really didn't know what to do. He knew he shouldn't leave the car, but he couldn't bear to stay in it. He opened the door, got out, and started running down the road in the direction from which they had come.

Within seconds, the rain soaked through his clothes and weighed him down. His feet sloshed in his shoes, and the intense rain blinded him. He lost all sense of direction, but he didn't really care.

He ran blindly down the road until there was a huge flash of light. Matthew screamed as he realized that he had been struck by lightning. After that, he remembered nothing, except that he felt very much at peace. A very bright and beautiful white light comforted him as nothing ever had before.

Matthew could hear a clear but gentle voice say, "Not yet, child. There is much work you have yet to do." Then he fell into a deep sleep.

Chapter 2

In the Hospital

In his semiconscious state, Matthew saw brilliant flashes of light. Everything he thought of passed through his mind at rates he never dreamed were possible. One second he would be thinking of Sara and the storm, the next second he would be thinking about the lightning and the voice he heard, and the next second he would be thinking about his internship and all the mistakes he had made. Although these thoughts were flying through his mind at a fantastic rate, Matthew found he could keep up with them all and remember everything.

In the background, Matthew could hear voices, though he could say nothing. The voices were becoming clearer by the minute. Finally, he could clearly make out a woman's voice.

"Doctor, he seems to be coming around a little."

"What are his vitals?"

"Pulse 68, blood pressure 120/70."

"Excellent. When he comes around, let me know."

"Understood, Doctor."

A half an hour later, Matthew opened his eyes and saw a very pretty nurse in her early twenties with blonde hair and a beautiful smile. Her name badge said "Jennifer."

"Well, hello there, Dr. Carpenter. It's nice to see you awake," she said. "You've been through quite an ordeal. You're lucky to be alive."

Matthew opened his mouth and whispered, "I feel like I've been run over by a truck...make that two trucks."

"I'm sure that you do. Most people would have been killed instantly." Jennifer paused, knowing that she should say something else. When she collected her thoughts, she continued.

"I'm terribly sorry about your wife. I knew her quite well. She was a very nice person. We used to go to lunch on occasion. If there is anything I can do for you, please let me know."

Sensing the formalness in her voice, Matthew decided to try to make her feel more comfortable. With a great deal of effort, he whispered, "Thank you for all you've done. Actually, I've got a pretty mean headache—though your kindness is certainly making me forget about some of the pain for a while."

Jennifer blushed without knowing why, which was quite out of character for her. After all, she was a professional nurse, and as a professional you were not supposed to have feelings for your patients. There was something about this man that was attractive to her, but she couldn't quite place her finger on it yet. Maybe it was that this was her friend's husband and she felt responsible for his well-being. *Yes, that must be it*, she thought to herself. But somehow, in the back of her mind, she wasn't so sure.

Quite suddenly, she realized that she had paused for a whole thirty seconds without saying anything. Regaining her composure, yet not quite knowing what to say, she just blurted out, "Well, thank you doctor."

She needed time to think. Not wanting to embarrass herself anymore, she said, "I'll need to go get Dr. Gomez. He indicated that he wanted to see you once you were awake." With that, she left the room. A fellow nurse named Vicky met her in the hall and, seeing her face all flushed, spoke up.

"Jenny, are you OK? You look like a high school girl that just got a crush on a boy in her class after he smiled at her."

Jenny looked at her wide-eyed and replied, "Oh my gosh! Is it that obvious?"

Vicky looked at her with one of those sarcastic looks. "Oh yeah! Big time!"

Jenny decided that it would be best to spend another few minutes composing herself before going to see Dr. Gomez.

Matthew was quite awake by this time and was looking around for something to do when he heard people at the door. Jennifer walked in with what he assumed was a doctor. The man was in his late forties and had a stethoscope around his neck.

"Well, Dr. Carpenter," said Dr. Gomez. "We're going to do a quick brain scan to see if there is any damage. Then, if everything is OK, we'll hold you for another twenty-four hours to make sure you're stable before we release you."

"How long have I been unconscious?"

"Three days."

"Three days? So…what's happened in the last few days since the accident? Has there been a funeral for my wife yet?"

"I'm afraid that was this afternoon at two P.M."

Matthew looked downcast, and both Jennifer and Dr. Gomez realized it. "Just my luck to have slept right through it," he said. "I'm guessing that's where all the family is."

Attempting to be comforting, Dr. Gomez reached out to place his hand on Matthew's, but immediately he recoiled as if in pain. He had received quite a shock—in fact, the biggest shock he had ever received in his life.

Dr. Gomez was taken aback by this and sarcastically said, "Hold on, there. What did I do to you?"

"Sorry, doc."

"No reason to apologize. This wasn't any fault of your own."

Jennifer left the room and then came back a minute later with several male nurses. They transferred Matthew to a gurney for transport to the lab. After a few minutes, they reached the lab and wheeled Matthew into the room where the scan was to take place.

"Just relax, Dr, Carpenter, and we'll be done in no time," said the technician in the lab. Her nametag said "Pamela."

Matthew smiled and with one raised eyebrow replied, "I don't think I'll be going anywhere for at least a few minutes." They both laughed.

Once Matthew was prepared for the test, Pamela went into a little room off to the side that was filled with equipment. Once she was set, she spoke to Matthew over the intercom.

"Are you ready, doctor?"

"All set, Pamela."

"Stay still and hold your breath. On the count of three, I'm going to take a picture. One, two, three."

They repeated this procedure several more times before the tests were finally completed. After a few minutes, Matthew looked over to the small room and noticed that Pamela was staring at the monitor in amazement. A minute later, he again heard her voice over the intercom.

"Dr. Gomez, report to room L-21. Dr. Gomez, report to room L-21."

Matthew never was one for surprises. He decided to try to get Pamela's attention. "Pamela!" he called out. "What's the problem?"

Pamela looked at Matthew from the other side of the glass and replied, "I haven't seen readings like this before. I need Dr. Gomez to interpret this."

Matthew was starting to get a bit panicked. "Interpret what? How about if I come take a look?"

"You know that's not allowed, doctor. Just wait for Dr. Gomez. He won't be long."

About five minutes later, Dr. Gomez came into the lab and looked at the monitor. He positioned his glasses on his nose so that he could view the monitor either with or without them. The doctor and technician talked for a few minutes, and then Dr. Gomez came out of the adjoining room and walked over to Matthew.

"I have never seen anything like this before," said Dr. Gomez. "Your brain activity is off the scale. We'll need to keep you around for a couple of days to see what this is all about."

"Hold on, doc. I don't intend to stay here any longer than I have to."

"You're a doctor. If you were in my shoes, you'd say the same thing."

Matthew started to again protest, but then realized that Dr. Gomez was right. He finally resigned himself and said, "Yeah, you're right."

Dr. Gomez thought for a few seconds. "You've made amazing progress, and there are no signs of tumors or other damage. Well, I at least want you to stay until you're back on your feet. Tell you what—I'll release you tomorrow on one condition."

"What's that?"

"You promise to come back if you feel anything out of the ordinary."

Matthew agreed, and Dr. Gomez left the room. Jennifer and the male nurses soon reappeared and placed Matthew back on the gurney. They wheeled Matthew to his room and helped him get back into his hospital bed.

Jennifer was still feeling strange around Matthew, but knew she had to do her job. So she spoke up in an exceedingly professional manner and said, "My shift is almost done. Is there anything I can do for you before I leave?"

"I feel like reading," Matthew replied. "Can you find me some medical textbooks so that I can catch up on a few technical tidbits? Some books on robotics, a few science fiction novels, or anything else you can find to read would also be fine."

Jennifer had never seen such progress in a patient before. It was as if his body was working on overdrive in the repair process. Although she wanted to stay and talk to him, she realized that would not be in the best interest of anyone—at least for now. So she simply said, "I'll see what I can find in the library here," and walked out.

Matthew started feeling much stronger and decided to sit up in the bed. Still feeling OK, he attempted to stand. As a doctor, he knew enough to hold on to something so that he wouldn't fall over, so he grabbed the railing on the bed to stabilize himself as he stood up. He could see very clearly and didn't feel tired at all. He walked over to the window and peered outside. It was very strange; although, he had just been through a terrible ordeal, he never physically felt this good before in his life. While he was marveling about how he felt, Jennifer walked back into the room.

"What are you doing up, Dr. Carpenter? You should be in bed."

"I feel just fine. In fact, I feel better than fine. I've never felt this good in my life. I can see perfectly both far or near, I can hear clearer than I ever have, and I don't feel tired at all."

"I don't care how you feel, you shouldn't be up like this."

Realizing that she had just put her foot in her mouth, she decided to rephrase her response. "Whoops, I didn't quite mean it that way. I meant that I care about my patients, and I don't want them getting up any sooner than they should. You should ask for help the first time you get up."

Smiling at her with one of those *thanks for thinking about me* looks, Matthew just said, "Thank you for your concern, mom."

Jennifer looked at him with a schoolgirl smile and shook her head—and then blushed again when she realized that she had given this look to him. She knew that she needed to quickly leave the room again, so she simply said, "Here are the books you asked for. I was able to find a couple of medical texts, a book on robotics, and some medical journals."

"Thank you so much, Jennifer. Will I see you tomorrow?"

"Bright and early at six A.M. I've got to go now. I'm volunteering at Awana tonight."

"So, you're a believer? I kind of thought so. Must be a sixth sense or something. I became a believer when I was thirteen years old. Smartest thing I ever did. Well, it looks like we have something in common."

Jennifer blushed even more than before. "I guess we do." Then she darted out of the room before she completely went to pieces.

Vicky saw her in the hall and, seeing that she was blushing yet again, yelled out, "Hey schoolgirl!"

"It's not funny. I'm so embarrassed. I think I've got a crush on him."

"At least you've realized it. But you need to be careful—I think everyone else in the hospital is realizing it as well. You need to watch out. He just lost his wife. Make sure you're not playing the hero and trying to fill a void."

Jennifer looked at her friend and smiled.

"I understand. Thanks."

Matthew picked up one of the journals and began flipping through the pages. Remarkably, as he did so he was able to read and retain all the information in it. He managed to read the entire journal in five minutes. He did the same for all the journals and all the books. When he had finished, he didn't even feel tired.

He decided to do some calisthenics. A few jumping jacks, deep knee bends, squats thrusts, and a few other isometrics. He was so happy with how he felt that he clapped his hands together. Immediately sparks flew from his hands, as if they had built up an extreme amount of static electricity. This surprised him to no end and caused him to sit down on the bed for a while.

After he calmed down, Matthew started thinking about what to do with his life. He thought for a few minutes and then decided to turn on the TV and catch up with what was going on in the world. Just his luck, the first thing that flickered on to the screen was a weather report. He was about to flip the channel, but then he saw that a massive category five hurricane was approaching off the coast of South Carolina. It was heading northwest at fifteen miles per hour.

"The eye of the hurricane is 120 miles southeast of Charleston," said the newscaster. "The winds are currently at 165 miles per hour, and the shoreline already looks like a disaster area. Reports from our local mobile unit show major destruction."

Matthew turned off the TV. He knew what he had to do. He tried to find his clothes, but then realized that he didn't have any. So he walked out to the nurse's station and asked about his clothes. The nurse on duty told him that his clothes were in the closet under some other personal items that his family had brought to him when he was unconscious.

Matthew went back to his room, dressed himself and then returned to the nurse's station. He saw that the name on her badge read "Cathy."

"Nurse Cathy, I'm checking myself out of the hospital. Tell Dr. Gomez that I'm leaving. Also, please leave a note for Jennifer saying that I'd like to keep in touch and that I'm sorry for leaving without a personal goodbye. Here is my cell phone number."

"Dr. Gomez isn't going to like this, Dr. Carpenter."

"Do you have a release form here that I can sign to get you off the hook?"

"Way ahead of you, doctor. Here you go."

Matthew took the release form, signed it and handed it back to the nurse.

"Thank you, nurse. Goodbye."

As Matthew was leaving, Vicky saw him out of the corner of her eye and said, "Dr. Carpenter, where are you going?" Matthew turned around and saw a nurse about Jennifer's age with curly brown hair coming toward him. "I'm a friend and coworker of Jennifer's," Vicky said when she had caught up with him.

"I've checked myself out of the hospital," Matthew replied. "I feel so good that there's no point in me staying here any longer. I'll try to keep in touch with Jennifer if I can, but at the moment I've got a mission to do, so I need to leave right away."

Vicky was caught by surprise. Before she knew what she was saying, she put her foot in her mouth, just like Jennifer had. "Jennifer is expecting to see you in the morning, and she'll be pretty hurt if you're gone."

"Please apologize for me. I'll contact her when I've returned."

With that, Matthew turned around and left the hospital.

Chapter 3

The Disaster Area

When Matthew arrived home, he decided to check on his car, which was being repaired at a local body shop.

"Dick's Auto Body," said the voice on the other end of the line. "Can I help you?"

"I'm Matthew Carpenter. I've got a gold four-door Impala in for repair. Can you give me some idea of when it'll be done?"

"It'll be at least three weeks. We've got a pretty big backlog, and we haven't got all your parts in yet."

"Three weeks! Is there anything I can do to get it sooner?"

"Well, you could pay all the folks here overtime and maybe get it back in a week once we get all the parts in."

"How soon before you expect the parts?"

"Supplier says it'll be at least a week and a half before they all get in."

"So, a week and a half to get the parts and another week to get it done. That's two and a half weeks. So all that I would really gain is about two to three days?"

"That's about right, buddy. Sorry, there's not much more I can do."

"OK, thanks for your time. I'll talk to you in about three weeks. Goodbye."

Matthew thought for a minute and then decided to check on renting a car. After thinking about it for a minute, he realized that a heavy-duty vehicle would be the best idea. The last thing he wanted was to get stuck in a disaster area and end up being part of the problem instead of the solution.

"What's the most rugged SUV you have in stock at the moment?" he asked the agent when he called the car rental company.

"I'm sorry, sir, but we don't have any SUVs available right now."

"When do you expect to have them in again?"

"The earliest would be at about this time tomorrow."

"Do any of the other branches have one available?"

"If you'll hold for a moment sir, I'll check."

"I'll hold."

The background music began to play a song that Matthew hadn't heard in a long time. It was the song that he and Sara had heard on their first date. The song brought a flood of memories back to him about the times that he and Sara had spent together. He felt the tears begin to well up in his eyes, but then the music abruptly stopped and the agent came back on the line.

"Our airport branch has a Hummer H2. They could get it here within an hour, if you'd like."

"That would be perfect. I'll be by in about an hour. Thank you for your effort. Goodbye."

"You're welcome sir. Good..."

Matthew hung up the phone before the agent could even finish the sentence. He took a cab to the rental car office and arrived a few minutes after the Hummer had arrived. He quickly made the arrangements in the office and headed outside to get into the big SUV. He had never driven a vehicle like this before, and it was a bit awkward for him at first.

After driving home to get some food and clothes, Matthew stopped by the local medical supply store to stock up on medical supplies. Being a doctor, he was able to obtain a few supplies that the average person wouldn't have been able to get—with or without a prescription.

When he finally thought that he was ready, he headed out for the disaster area. Matthew lived about 200 miles to the northwest of what was likely to be the closest area in need. He decided that it would be best to fill up with fuel as often as he could, as he didn't really know when the power would go out and he'd be on his own.

Matthew had a lot of time to think during his 200-mile journey. He thought about his family, Sara's family, the good and the bad times that he and Sara had experienced together and, of course, about the accident. As he got closer to the hurricane area, he began to see fallen trees, downed power lines and flooded streets in the low-lying areas. He was glad that he had made the effort to get the Hummer, because the big SUV made a real difference as to what he could get through. After another sixty miles, he started to see many people who appeared to be very dazed and wandering aimlessly. It was apparent from their wretched state that they had all been through quite an ordeal. Matthew knew that it would be a very long time before that area would be back to normal.

One particular man caught his eye. He was a middle-aged gentleman who was sitting down on a wooden crate near the side of the road. Seeing the total despair in his face, Matthew decided to pull over to help him.

"Is there anything I can help you with?" he said. "I'm a doctor."

The gentleman looked up and after a few seconds said, "My house is gone, my wife is dead, and my two kids are lost. I just don't know what to do." Matthew began to realize that this was not going to be as easy as he first thought.

"Show me where your wife is, where you last saw your children, and what they look like. Oh, by the way, what's your name?"

"My name is Jonathan Wilder. The remains of my house are right over there." Jonathan pointed to a pile of sticks and rubble about 200 feet behind him. "I happened to get out of the house just before it collapsed a couple of hours ago. I found my wife around the back with a tree on top of her. I never did find the kids. The kids were supposed to be in the house asleep. I have a boy, Tim, who's ten, and a girl, Anna, who's eight."

Jonathan stood up, and the two of them walked over to where the tree had fallen on his wife. As Matthew approached the back of what used to be Jonathan's house, he could see a figure lying on the ground about fifty feet ahead of him with a fifteen-inch tree limb across her back. He immediately ran over to her and checked her vitals. As near he could tell, the woman had been dead for about four hours. Her back was broken and she had multiple compound fractures.

Matthew knew that there was nothing he could do for her now, so he slowly stood up and walked back toward the house. As he observed the collapsed structure, he noticed that there was a rear bulkhead on the house, which meant that there was a basement. Clearing away some of the debris, he found the doors, carefully opened them, and then walked down the stairs. The door to the basement was splintered and was not very hard to push open. When he reached the bottom of the stairs, he turned on a small flashlight that he had previously placed in his pocket. His heart immediately sank.

Near the middle of the basement, he saw a boy who had appeared to be crushed by a fallen beam. Near him, there was a girl who appeared to be unconscious. Matthew rushed over to them and checked for vitals. The boy was clearly dead, but the girl was alive. One of the beams had crushed her legs, but other than that, she appeared to be all right.

"Anna! Anna! Can you hear me?"

The girl moaned and appeared to be very groggy. With some effort, Matthew lifted the beam off of her and looked at her legs. One of her legs was broken and the other one was mangled beyond repair. He quickly ran out to the SUV and grabbed his medical supplies. On his way back, he found Jonathan, who was sitting beside his wife, and told him that his daughter was alive.

Jonathan got up and ran along with Matthew to the basement. When he saw his daughter, he bent over her and started crying.

"I'm going to need your help, Jonathan," said Matthew. "I want you to try to talk to your daughter and keep her awake. Just don't tell her anything that will get her any more upset than she already is. I'm going to give her a shot for pain, which will numb her legs for a while so that I can look at them a little closer."

As Matthew gave her a couple of shots and immobilized what was left of her legs, Jonathan talked to Anna. "Anna, sweetheart," he said, "Daddy's here."

"Daddy, how's Mommy and Timmy?"

Jonathan didn't know what to say. "We'll see, darling. Right now, this doctor here is going to see if he can help you."

Anna started to cry. "Daddy, I'm scared. I can't feel my legs."

Jonathan held her hand, stroked her long blonde hair and kissed her forehead. "The doctor is going to do all he can for you."

"Anna, I've given you some medicine to help with the pain," said Matthew. "We'll get you to a hospital. You're going to be all right. OK?"

"Will I be able to walk again?"

For the first time in his life, Matthew didn't know what to say. He glanced down at the girl's legs and realized there wasn't much he could do for the right one. The left one looked salvageable. All he could say was, "I'll do what I can, Anna."

Matthew realized that he had made a mistake in coming out there by himself. He could have really used some additional medical support. Although he had lots of supplies, he had not thought much about the logistics of only being able to work on one patient at a time. He would have to go all the way back to a place that had power and drop off Anna before he could consider trying to help anyone else.

The two men picked up Anna and placed her on the stretcher that Matthew had brought. They then carried her to the SUV and put her in the back. Matthew had at least brought a long-range two-way radio that was patched in to most emergency services. He tuned the radio to the band that he knew was monitored by medical personnel.

"Emergency medical, this is Dr. Matthew Carpenter. Can anyone read me?"

"We read you, Dr. Carpenter. This is Florence General. What is your location?"

"Close to Conway. Do you copy?"

"Loud and clear."

"I've got a girl, eight years old, left leg fracture, right leg crushed. I've stabilized her and will be in route to you shortly. What's the quickest way to Florence?"

"Go up route 501. I expect that it will take you a couple of hours."

"Understood, Florence. Over and out."

Jonathan stayed in the back with Anna and talked to her as Matthew headed to Florence. Matthew checked on them occasionally to make sure that everything was fine. He had given Anna enough medication to keep her relatively pain free until they arrived at the hospital.

Much of the way to Florence, Matthew was haunted by Anna's words: "Doctor, will I be able to walk again… Doctor, will I be able to walk again…Doctor, will I be able to walk again?" The words rang over and over in Matthew's head until he couldn't take it any longer.

Suddenly his head began to tingle, much like it had when he read all those books in a matter of minutes, and hundreds of equations and formulas raced through his head. It was the most incredible feeling he had ever experienced in his life. Things that he never thought possible all of a sudden became quite clear to him. When his mind stopped racing, he had a picture of what he needed to do. He had to create a machine that would automatically analyze what was wrong with a person, disassemble the person into pieces that could be easily managed, eliminate or repair any bad parts, clone any other parts that would be necessary to help in the repair, and then reassemble the person. In essence, he would invent a device that would be able to take Anna's good left leg, clone it and make her a new right leg. He couldn't wait to start building it. But first, he knew that he had to concentrate on the problem at hand.

As Matthew approached Florence, he saw a sign with a blue "H" and decided that it was time to offer a few words of encouragement. "Anna, we're almost there, honey," he said. "We'll see if we can get you some ice cream in a little while."

Matthew continued to follow the blue H signs and within another few minutes he had located the hospital. There had been some wind damage in the area, but the hospital itself seemed to be in pretty good condition. He drove up to the emergency entrance, got out of the SUV, and went into the hospital to get some help. Two men followed him out and helped to pull Anna out. Jonathan never left her side. Matthew parked the SUV in a more suitable spot and went back into the emergency entrance. Once there, he located a social worker and explained the situation to her, telling her that she needed to contact FEMA and arrange counseling for both Anna and Jonathan due to the loss of Anna's mother, brother and home. After that, he went back to check on Anna and Jonathan.

"I've already talked to a social worker about contacting FEMA for your home and about arranging some counseling for the both of you," Matthew said to Jonathan.

"Thank you, Dr. Carpenter."

Matthew decided next that it was time to talk to the head ER doctor, so he had the nurse page him. "I'm Dr. Matthew Carpenter from the Charlotte area," he said when the ER doctor appeared. "How's Anna doing?"

"I'm Dr. Jim Skyler. I've managed to set Anna's left leg, and we're about to place a cast on it. Her right leg is not salvageable below the knee. We'll have to amputate. Good thing you called in—we were able to have everything ready for you when you got here. Another few hours and we'd have had to take more off than that."

"Is there anything I can do?"

"Yes, you can get some sleep and keep Anna's father company. The nurse can tell you what room she will be in. It will be at least a couple of hours before the surgery is complete and she can get back to her room."

"Although I really don't feel tired, you're right—I should probably take care of Mr. Wilder."

Matthew talked to the nurse and found out that Anna was to be in room 221. He and Jonathan went to Anna's room, and Matthew did some reading while Jonathan slept.

Matthew closed his eyes to think about what he should do once he left the hospital. His mind started racing again. Lists of parts ran through his mind, and he realized that these were the parts that he would need for his invention. He quickly asked the nurse for some paper and started writing out the list of things that he would have to buy. By the time he was through, Dr. Skyler came into the room with Anna, who was sedated.

"I think she'll be just fine," he said. "It'll be eight weeks before her left leg will be healed enough for her to walk on with crutches. It would usually take six weeks, but because that leg will be the one that has to carry all the weight, it'll take a little longer. She'll be here for about a week so that we can verify there isn't any infection. Hopefully, by that time the social workers and FEMA will have found these two a place to live."

"Jonathan was an engineer with SIMUTECKNIK," said Matthew. "He can attempt to contact them, but I don't think he'll have any luck until the power is restored in the area. Give it about a week, and things may be in a little better shape. He'll have some bereavement time anyway, due to the loss of two family members."

Matthew waited another few hours until both Anna and Jonathan were awake and then said his goodbyes.

"Will I see you again, doctor?" asked Anna.

"I expect so. I'll check in on you every so often. I expect that the hospital, FEMA or SIMUTECKNIK should be able to track you down. Goodbye, Anna. Goodbye, Jonathan."

"Thank you so much for everything, doctor," said Jonathan. "You saved my daughter's life."

"You're very welcome. I'm a sucker for little girls, and just seeing her back alive and in better shape than when we found her is reward enough for me. Goodbye."

Matthew left the hospital and got in his Hummer for the long ride home. As he was driving, he first thought about his invention and then about Jennifer.

"Oh, boy. I just met the girl and I'm probably already in the doghouse. I feel like I should pursue her, and yet I just lost Sara. I really don't know what I should do. Only time will tell. I'll pray about it on the way home. Perhaps the Lord will shed some light on this mess."

Chapter 4

The Project

When Matthew arrived home, he thought it best to give his apologies to Jennifer as soon as possible. There was no use letting things get any worse than they probably already were. So he called the hospital and found out that Jennifer would be on duty that night starting at six P.M. It was four P.M., so he would probably not arrive there until at least seven P.M.

On the way he started thinking more and more about the machine idea, and again his mind started to race as more equations screamed through his head. What was odd was that he could keep up with every one of them and remember them with great detail.

At seven fifteen he arrived at the hospital and found Jennifer at one of the nurse's stations. When she saw him she started to leave, but Matthew caught her arm. She felt all tingly when he touched her, just like the times she was interested in boys when she was a teenager.

"I apologize for leaving so suddenly," said Matthew. "I should have left you a personal note instead of letting others do the dirty work. I just came back from South Carolina, where I rescued a family displaced from the hurricane and managed to save the life of an eight-year-old girl. Again, I'm sorry for leaving so suddenly."

For a moment, Jennifer didn't know what to say. She didn't know whether to be angry or whether she was just happy to see him alive. She needed time to think. It was obvious that he had some interest in her, and yet some time might do them both good. In the end, she decided to remain aloof and see what would eventually happen. She might regret it later, but she thought it best to take the chance.

"Well, I'm just glad to see that you're all right, Dr. Carpenter. If you'll excuse me, I've got some patients to attend to."

With that, Jennifer went down the hall toward one of her patient's rooms. As she went tears started to form in her eyes, and by the time she reached the room they were streaming down her face. She felt really bad for treating Matthew the way that she had, but she needed time to think.

Matthew was caught by surprise and didn't quite know what to think. All he knew was that he did the right thing. Maybe he'd call her in a week or so, after she'd cooled down a little.

Back home, Matthew became totally absorbed in working on his machine. He decided to write the software first, as that would allow him to think about what sensors and other interfaces would later be required. He decided to use his laptop to do this because it had a very large screen, an independent keyboard and mouse, and gave him the flexibility to use a larger separate monitor when necessary. He could also take the basic laptop with him wherever he went. Luckily, he already had a C++ compiler installed on the laptop.

What Matthew found interesting was that he wasn't tired at all, even though he hadn't slept a wink since he woke up in the hospital a week ago. He wrote code for hours on end and for weeks at a time, yet to him the time passed very quickly. To anyone watching, his pace would have seemed like something out of a superhero movie—his fingers were moving at such a rapid rate that you couldn't really keep up with them. The only thing Matthew took breaks for were to get something to eat and to hit the bathroom.

By the time the program was complete, Matthew had created more than a million lines of code. He decided to find what day it was. After realizing that about fifteen weeks had passed, he thought it was high time that he check on Anna.

He gave Florence General Hospital a call and found out that FEMA had put Anna and Jonathan up in a trailer near their previous home in Conway. With a little more digging, he found a number at which he could reach them.

"Hello," came a little girl's voice over the line that sounded like Anna.

"Hi Anna, this is Dr. Carpenter. I figured I'd check on you. How are you feeling, sweetheart?"

"Dad, it's Dr. Carpenter," the girl yelled to her father, who must have been close in the background. "I'm doing OK. I really miss mommy and Timmy, and I don't really like not being able to walk, but when some of my friends come by, I try to forget about my problems."

Matthew didn't know what to say. He fumbled with his words and at last replied, "I'm just glad you're alive, sweetie. Can I talk to your daddy for a minute?"

Jonathan picked up the phone. "Hello Dr. Carpenter. I just want to thank you for all you did. Thanks to you, I have my little girl back. SIMUTECKNIK is back on line now and I'm back at work. I got a friend to watch Anna while I'm at work until she is ready to go back to school. Actually, they haven't started school yet, because the hurricane wiped the school away. I think they're planning on holding classes in trailers for some time to come, which should be ready to go in another week or so. Anna healed up quicker than the hospital expected and has managed to use crutches. She isn't exactly doing jumping jacks, but I'm happy to have her alive."

"Well, that's good news. Give her a big hug for me. I'll be in touch. Goodbye."

Matthew obviously couldn't do anything about Anna's mother or brother, but he realized that he just might be able to do something for Anna.

Soon, all of the parts that Matthew had ordered for the machine began to arrive in boxes at his house, and he began the laborious task of putting it together. About a week later, the phone rang.

"Hello," he said.

"Hi, Matthew," the voice on the other end of the line replied. "It's Jennifer."

There was a dead silence for about five seconds, and then Jennifer got the courage to speak up.

"I'm sorry for acting so childish. It's been eating at me for the last several months. I really shouldn't have been so cold."

"That's OK. A lot has been happening to me lately, and I didn't realize it had been so long since I was in the hospital."

Again there was a dead silence for about ten seconds, and then Jennifer again broke in.

"I know it's only been a few months since your wife passed away, but I was wondering if you'd like to have dinner with me tomorrow? I know a great little Polynesian restaurant a few miles from my house."

Matthew was totally speechless.

Hearing no response, Jennifer started getting worried and wondered if she made a mistake by calling him. After a couple of deep breaths, she decided that she had come this far and was determined to follow through even if he never spoke to her again. After all, it would have been only fair after the way she treated him. After about fifteen seconds, Jennifer followed up, "If you really don't want to, just say so and I won't bother you again."

"No, it's not that," Matthew finally replied. "I'm sorry I didn't answer earlier. I would really love to have dinner with you. By the way, I don't even know your last name."

"It's Tucker. Well, then, I'll pick you up at six P.M. tomorrow."

"Do you know where I live?"

"I'm pretty resourceful. I'll figure it out. Goodnight."

"Goodnight."

Matthew was still in shock and didn't know what to think. Could he really be interested in someone else so soon after his wife had died?

He set an alarm for five P.M. the next day just in case he was working too hard and lost track of the time. By the time five P.M. rolled around, he had finished building the machine and was ready to load the software. But that would have to wait until after his date. He decided to take a shower and clean up, as he didn't exactly look or smell the best from all the continuous work.

Six o'clock came pretty quickly, and as he was putting his shoes on he heard a knock at the door. When he opened it, all he could do was stare. Jennifer had her blonde hair down, and it flowed down over her shoulders. She was wearing a beautiful long blue dress with a white shawl.

"Well, are you just going to keep me on the porch, or are you going to invite me in?"

"I'm sorry, I was just admiring your dress. Please come in. I was just finishing tying my shoes when you knocked. All I need is to grab a jacket and I'll be ready."

Matthew quickly grabbed his coat and headed out the door, at which point he hesitated. "I'll drive if you tell me where I'm going," he said.

"I'm parked in back of you, so I may as well drive."

Matthew looked at Jennifer, shook his head and replied, "I'm getting the better end of the bargain on this deal already." He opened her car door and closed it after she was seated.

"So, you know a whole lot more about me than I know about you," Matthew said when they were underway. "How about if you tell me a little bit about yourself?"

"Let's see, where to start? I was born in the hills of Virginia. I was the only child of a farming family. Both of my parents died in an automobile accident soon after I graduated. That was only a few years ago. I went to North Carolina State, where I received my nursing degree, and I have been working in Charlotte ever since. I love the Lord, Awana, baby animals and helping people."

Jennifer took a deep breath as she decided what to say next. She wasn't sure whether to mention Sara or not, but she figured she would take a chance.

"I worked with Sara for a few years. We were very good friends. I'm surprised she didn't mention me to you at all."

"She could have, but with trying to get through school and interning, I probably didn't pay as much attention to what she was saying as I should have." Matthew paused for a moment.

"I had put all that out of my mind for the last few months while I was working on my new project," he continued. "Eventually I'll have to come to grips with it. I'm sure that with the Lord's help, I'll get through it."

"You have the right attitude. At least you know that you can't do it without God. It takes most people all their lives to realize that. In fact, some people never realize it."

They both sat there for a minute feeling rather somber. Then Jennifer spoke up again.

"Anyway, I really like working with the people at the hospital. The patients are so interesting. I get them to talk about themselves, and it cheers them up. It's really good therapy for them."

They arrived at the Polynesian restaurant a few minutes later. Once they were seated and had a chance to look at the menu for a few minutes, Matthew spoke up.

"How daring are you?"

"Uh…it depends. What do you have in mind?"

"What do you think about this surprise special dinner for two?"

"Hey, we're out to have fun so…sure, I'm game."

"Great."

They both had a marvelous meal. As the night progressed, they each began talking about funny or embarrassing moments that had happened in their lives.

"So I got down to the hurricane area to help lots of people," said Matthew, "and as I was finishing up with Anna and her father, I realized that I had to go all the way to a hospital that had power to drop her off before I could do anything else. Talk about poor planning!"

They both laughed, and then Jennifer had her chance.

"I was once in charge of the Cubbies activities at a big Awana event. I was supposed to go on stage in a few minutes with them. One of the little girls I had was a precious three year old. She didn't want to go on stage and started to cry. So I took her on my lap and tried to console her. The next thing I knew, my lap felt awful warm."

Matthew broke in, "No...she didn't, did she?"

"Yup! Peed all over my lap. I was dripping! It was all over the floor, and neither of us had any extra clothes."

"So what happened next?"

"Well, I called back to one of the Awana leaders to run to the kitchen and grab some of the hand towels that were there. Within sixty seconds, I had half a dozen hand towels. My friend took the little girl and started wiping her up. I used a couple on myself and the rest on the floor. I asked one of the older women in the group to see if she could find a kitchen apron around anywhere. Within a couple of minutes, she was back with a full apron. I looked at it, and she just shrugged her shoulders."

"What was wrong with it?"

"On the apron was a huge hen with baby chicks. You'd have to have seen it to fully appreciate it. Anyway, just after I put it on, we were called up on the stage. Everything turned out fine in the end, but I was pretty self-conscious for a while until everything had dried. There's nothing like a little *Water on the Knee* to fully appreciate a shower at night."

They both roared with laughter for a good thirty seconds.

After Matthew paid the bill, they got back in the car for the ride home. On their way, Matthew looked up and saw a young puppy no more than a couple of months old dart across the road about one hundred feet in front of them. The dog barely missed the driver's side front wheel of an oncoming car, but the automobile smacked it and ran right over the top of it. Jennifer screamed and slammed on her brakes. The other automobile drove off as Jennifer came to a stop.

They both jumped out of the car and examined the dog. It was still alive, but it had a pretty bad head injury and likely numerous internal injuries. Matthew realized that the puppy would probably only survive another few hours.

"I don't think there is anything we can do for him," said Jennifer.

"Based on the extent of his injuries, I expect he's only got one chance," replied Matthew.

"What do you mean? There's nothing that can be done for him—even if we were able to get the best vet at this time of night."

Matthew just glanced over at Jennifer with an odd look on his face. It was one of those looks you give when you've resolved in your own mind the best solution to a dilemma.

"I built a machine at home that could probably heal him. I was about to load the software when I had to get ready to come out with you for dinner."

"You did what? What are you talking about?"

"Looks like the only way to convince you will be to bring the dog back to my workshop and show you."

Matthew carefully picked up the unconscious puppy and laid him in the back seat of the car. Although the dog was seriously injured, the bleeding had slowed down. Always the nurse, Jennifer had a blanket in the car that they used to place the puppy on—that would at least keep the car from getting too messy. The two got into the car and Matthew starting driving to his house. Neither of them spoke on the way, but Jennifer looked at Matthew with a very curious and fearful look. She wanted to say something, but she really didn't know what. She thought it best to keep quiet rather than stick her foot in her mouth.

When they got to the house, Matthew threw Jennifer the house keys and carefully pulled the puppy out of the back seat. Jennifer opened the house door and followed Matthew to the workshop.

Matthew's house was a ranch style with three bedrooms, two full baths, a living room, a family room, a full basement and a garage converted to a workshop, where Matthew had been working on his invention. When she turned the light on, her jaw dropped as she saw the maze of wiring and computer equipment. In the middle of the room was a funny-looking contraption that she couldn't identify. Half-afraid and half-curious, she just stayed in the doorway for the first few minutes.

Matthew laid the puppy on a platform inside the machine and closed a glass door. He quickly fired up the computer and loaded the application software. The download only took about a minute, and then Matthew spent another few minutes doing some system configuring. After finishing the configuration, he was ready for the test—although he had never expected that the first test would be so critical.

Matthew took a deep breath and closed his eyes. "OK, here goes nothing."

He applied power to the machine and it quickly ran through its internal test mode. Once it completed, the monitor indicated a ready state.

"Abby, are you with us?" Matthew said to the machine.

"All circuits online and functional," a voice replied.

"Good. Analyze the patient."

"Acknowledged."

Fifteen seconds later, a voice came back from the computer speakers. "Patient has severe internal bleeding, torn small intestine, lacerated left kidney, severe liver damage and numerous lacerations to the head."

Matthew took a deep breath. "OK, Abby. Disassemble and repair."

"Acknowledged."

Jennifer had been looking over Matthew's shoulder for the last few minutes, watching as the computer interacted with Matthew. As she looked at the body of the dog, she suddenly saw a flash and the body disappear. "What happened to the puppy!" she screamed.

"With any luck, I'd say it's about to be repaired."

A voice again came over the computer speakers. "Time for repair is two minutes, thirty-two seconds."

Matthew turned to speak with Jennifer. "The computer, which I call Abby, disassembles and stores all the molecules of the patient. It then deletes bad cells, clones and repairs others, and then reassembles the patient. The only drawback is that this can only be performed once in a patient's life. This is due to the fact that the machine slightly alters the patient's chemical make-up to allow the new cells to be accepted. Once the body gets used to this change, it sets up a defense mechanism to disallow it from happening again."

Although Jennifer was in a complete daze, she knew that Matthew expected some sort of response from her, so she just blurted out, "That's incredible!"

After another minute, Abby came back with a statement about the next phase of the repair.

"Repair completed. Starting reassembly."

The next thing Jennifer saw was a bright flash, and then the puppy was back on the table. It picked its head up and started wagging its tail. Matthew got up, went over to the puppy and picked it up.

"He looks in pretty good shape. I think we can bring him back home, assuming we can figure out where his home is. Jennifer, could you take the puppy and see if you can find a dog tag or some means of identifying him? I should take a look at Abby to make sure that all the systems are functional and that nothing is out of the ordinary before I shut her down."

"Sure, Matthew."

Matthew quickly ran a few diagnostics to verify that everything was OK and then told Abby to power down. Jennifer found a dog tag and also a second tag identifying what the puppy's name was and where he lived. "Well, hello there, Max. You about ready to go home?"

Max looked at the humans with his mouth open and tongue hanging out. He wagged his tail and let out a couple of small barks.

Matthew and Jennifer left the house and eventually found the home of the puppy. They rang the doorbell, and two children about Anna's age came to the door. When they saw the puppy they were thrilled.

"Max, where have you been? We've been worried to death about you," said the little boy. "Thank you so much for finding him and bringing him home. We brought him outside and didn't put a leash on him. He saw a rabbit across the yard and made a mad dash for it. We tried to keep up with him, but we couldn't."

"You're welcome," replied Matthew. "As you can see, he's just fine." With that, Matthew and Jennifer left.

Jennifer couldn't stop talking all the way back to Matthew's house. "Do you know what this means? We could save lots of people's lives. People with cancer, people with lost limbs, people who are infertile, people who are mentally disabled. The possibilities are endless."

"There are some limitations. I can't bring people who have been dead for a while back to life, and I can't erase people's memories of bad experiences. What I really want to do is get Anna back to being a normal little girl with two legs."

Jennifer looked at Matthew and in a loving voice responded, "She really means a lot to you, doesn't she?"

"Yeah, she did kind of tug at my heart a little. In any case, I'm going to go down there tomorrow and bring her back here to fix her up."

"Actually, tomorrow's Saturday, and I'm off until eight A.M. Sunday morning. So…can I help?"

Matthew thought about this for a few seconds and then said, "Are you serious about helping?"

"Of course!"

"Well…if you'd really like to help, what I really need is to have the house straightened up and for someone to make dinner for us. I could also use help to get one of the guest rooms prepared for Anna and Jonathan, just in case they want to stay the night. It's not a glorious job, but one that I really need done."

Jennifer looked at Matthew with a smart-aleck sort of look. "If I hadn't seen the condition of the house when I came in, I'd have said you were just trying to get rid of me. But…after seeing the true condition of it, I'm inclined to agree with you. I accept the task."

"Thanks. You're a real sport. Well, it's getting late—here's a key to the house. You can let yourself in when you get here in the morning, since I should be on the road by then. Even though I hate to see you go, you should probably get some sleep."

Jennifer looked at Matthew and smiled. As he opened the house door for her, she reached out for his hand and grabbed it. He turned his face toward her and she gave him a quick kiss. They looked at each other for a second, and then Matthew smiled and winked at her. He finished opening the door, and they said goodnight.

When Matthew was again inside the house, he picked up the phone and dialed the Wilders.

"Hello?" said a man at the other end of the line.

"Hello, this is Dr. Carpenter. Is this Jonathan?"

"Hello, doctor. It's great to hear from you."

"How's Anna doing?"

"She's trying to cope. It's hard for her when she sees all her friends running and playing."

"Do you have any plans for tomorrow?"

"No. We we're just going to try to do a little food shopping."

"If I came to get you, would you like to come up for a visit? I've got a surprise for her, but I can only give it to her here."

"It would really cheer up Anna to see you again. I'm sure that she'd like the adventure."

"Great, I'll pick you up at seven A.M. Go ahead and eat breakfast first."

"That will be excellent. We'll see you in the morning, doctor. Goodbye."

"Goodnight."

Matthew didn't quite know what to do at the moment. Before the accident he would have had to immediately go to bed in order to get up at about three thirty A.M. to get to Anna's by seven. But since he didn't need to sleep, he decided to just sit for a moment and pray.

"Lord, I'm not sure what You're planning for the rest of my life, but I'm open to whatever You have in mind. I praise You for all You have done for me and whatever You are doing through me. Please guide me in all Your ways and always get me to do what is right in Your sight."

As he was sitting there, his mind started flashing again. He saw Jennifer in a wedding dress, and he was standing next to her at an altar. He then saw a car accident.

"Lord, what is to happen? Will I marry Jennifer and then lose her like I lost Sara?"

Matthew felt a presence and what seemed to be a voice saying, "Do not be afraid. I am in control and everything will be all right. Jennifer will become your wife and shall bear you a daughter. She will be great in the sight of the Lord, and through her many will come to repentance. Her mind will be even greater than your own, and she will have power beyond your imagination."

Matthew's mind started racing again and new formulas and computations rushed through his head. Matthew realized that this new data would allow him to enhance his invention and fill in a couple of gaps. Specifically, the data would allow him to selectively delete memories from a person and, in certain cases, allow him to bring people back to life and restore their brain function. In some cases, he might even be able to enhance it.

Before he knew it, it was three thirty A.M. He cleaned himself up and was ready to get on the road by four A.M.

Seven hours later, Matthew pulled into the driveway with Jonathan and Anna. They all got out of the car, and then Anna walked with her crutches into the house. Jennifer met them at the door and indicated that dinner would be ready in another half an hour.

"That'll be just about enough time to square away Anna," said Matthew. "Come on Anna, we're going to see what we can do for your leg."

Jonathan looked at Matthew. "What are you talking about, doc?" he said.

"I've invented something that should help Anna walk. Jennifer, could you please help Anna get ready while I fire up Abby?"

"No problem."

Jennifer escorted Anna to the workshop while Matthew powered up the machine. Jennifer then helped Anna up onto the table and closed the door.

Matthew looked at Anna and, smiling, said, "Don't worry Anna, I'll take good care of you."

"I know that, doctor," said Anna. "By the way, could I get some ice cream for dessert?"

Everyone laughed, and then they all heard Abby say, "All systems functional." Being a technical person himself, Jonathan was very curious about the machine.

"What is this, doctor?"

"Abby is my computer. She's ready to work on Anna."

Jonathan looked at Matthew with a suspicious yet curious look.

"What do you mean 'work on'?"

"Abby is going to repair the damage from the accident."

"She's going to do *what*?"

"Don't worry, Jonathan. We've got everything under control. Abby, analyze the patient."

"Acknowledged," came the voice from the computer. "Patient has an amputated right leg, a small brain tumor and an ovarian cyst."

"Abby, can you confirm on the tumor and cyst?"

"Analyzing." A few seconds later, Abby came back with, "Confirmation complete."

"Jonathan, has Anna been complaining about any headaches lately?"

"Actually, she has."

"Very curious. We'll just have to wait and see. OK Abby, disassemble and repair."

Immediately there was a bright flash, and then Anna was gone. Jonathan was nearly frantic. "What happened to Anna!" he cried.

"It's going to be all right, Jonathan. Abby is repairing her. If all goes well, she should be as good as new in about five minutes from now. For the moment, we just wait. In the meantime, tell me how long Anna has had these headaches."

"I'd say about six weeks. I had been wondering if it was a result of the accident."

"It's quite possible. Wouldn't you agree, Jennifer?"

"I would say so," Jennifer replied. "If the trauma and the atmosphere in the basement were particularly bad, she could have developed a tumor, although I would not have expected to see it in her brain. By the way, how have all the other children in school and the neighborhood reacted to Anna? Have they accepted her pretty well?"

"Yes, very well. They all liked Anna before the accident, and they have all treated her more like a sister than somebody with a disability. I think it's because all of them were affected in some way by the hurricane."

"Well, that's terrific. With any luck, she should be as good as new pretty shortly."

Just then Abby blurted out, "Repair completed. Starting reassembly." There was another bright flash, and then Anna was back on the table in one piece. She opened her eyes, sat up on the table and with a huge smile on her face said, "Daddy! I have both legs, and they feel super! My headache is gone, too."

Jennifer opened the glass door and Anna jumped off the table. She ran to her father as he opened his arms and picked her up, spinning her around. The next thing they all knew, each of them were laughing and crying at the same time. Matthew gave Anna a big hug and held her for what seemed like an hour, though it was only a couple of minutes.

"Doctor?" asked Anna. "Can we eat now? I'm really hungry?"

All everyone could do was laugh.

After they ate, Matthew indicated that it was time for him to drive Jonathan and Anna back home. Jennifer said goodbye to them and then said to Matthew, "I'll see you later. I've got to be at work at eight A.M. but I'll see you after I get off work tomorrow night."

"Got yourself a deal."

Jennifer gave Matthew a kiss and they both parted ways. Anna was already outside doing jumping jacks and flips. She had a lot of built up energy that she was just raring to burn up.

When they got back to the FEMA trailer where Anna and Jonathan had been temporarily living, Anna saw some of her friends and quickly jumped out of the car. When her friends saw her, they all ran up to her and started screaming. They all wanted to know what happened, and then they started jumping around and dancing.

"Well, Jonathan, I can't see me staying here much longer. I'll just say my goodbyes now. Keep tabs on Anna and let me know if she has any problems. I believe she'll be just fine."

"Thank you so much for everything you've done for Anna and me. I owe you a lot, doc. If there's ever anything I can do for you, just let me know."

Matthew thought for a moment and then said, "I may eventually want to make some production runs of my invention. Maybe you could see if your company would be interested in a business venture."

"I'll talk to them first thing Monday morning and let you know."

"Thanks. I guess it won't be long before we'll be pulling that off. I'm sure my machine will sell like hotcakes."

Matthew and Jonathan shook hands and said goodbye one final time. Matthew saw Anna with her friends and yelled out, "Goodbye Anna!"

Anna turned to see who was talking and waved. "Bye, doctor!"

With that, Matthew got back in his car and went home.

Living Nightmare

When Matthew returned home, he immediately started working on the enhancements he had thought up. When he hadn't heard from Jennifer by nine P.M. Sunday night, he called her at home and on her cell phone. In each case he only got her voicemail, which he thought was quite strange. Once he finished the enhancements, he decided to call the hospital and try to locate her at the nurse's station that she normally reported to.

"Hello, this is Dr. Carpenter. May I speak to Nurse Tucker?"

"Oh, Dr. Carpenter. I guess you haven't heard—Jennifer was in a horrible accident with a drunk driver. She's currently in a coma. She's lost a leg, an arm, has numerous internal injuries and was burned over 25 percent of her body. Dr. Butler doesn't know whether she will make it."

Matthew couldn't speak for a minute.

"Dr. Carpenter?"

"Yes, I'm sorry. I'm just in shock, that's all. I'll be right over. Thanks for the information. Goodbye."

"Goodbye, doctor."

Matthew was totally heartbroken. He thought that he and Jennifer would get married some day. Then he remembered! "What am I thinking? God Himself told me that Jennifer and I would have a daughter. Think, Matthew, think. She's on life support. I can't just walk in there and take her home to Abby. What can I do to save her?" The room started spinning and his mind began racing again. Formulas upon formulas raced through his head.

"A portable unit? Yes, that would work—but how could I build that in a matter of hours? Let's see, I've got material enough to make another disassembler. If I scrounge up enough parts, maybe I can come up with a way to transport particles over to Abby and back again."

Matthew spent the next twelve hours writing some extra code that would allow Abby to import transmitted particles and retransmit them. He also built a simple transmit/receive antenna for Abby and a unit that could be aimed at a person, disassemble him or her, transmit that person to Abby and then reassemble him or her once the repairs had been made.

"Good thing I just wrote that extra code," he said to himself. "It might come in handy about now."

Once Matthew finished the machine, which was only about the size of a small rifle, he headed for the hospital. Once he arrived, he headed for her room in the intensive care unit. When he was within earshot, he noticed a great deal of commotion coming from the place where Jennifer was supposed to be. When he got within about ten feet, he saw a number of people standing around Jennifer's bed and a lot of resuscitation equipment in the room. He overheard some of the nurses and doctors talking.

"We're losing her, doctor," said one of the nurses.

Thirty seconds later, the monitor flat-lined. Immediately the attending doctor shouted, "Let's shock her, *stat!*"

The nurse came back a few seconds later with an external defibrillator. Once the unit had fully charged, the doctor placed two big pads on Jennifer, one on her chest and one toward her back.

"Ready doctor," said the attending nurse.

"Now!" shouted the doctor.

Jennifer's chest jolted up.

"Again!"

Jennifer's chest jolted up again.

"Again!"

Jennifer's chest jolted up a third time.

"It's no use, doctor, she's gone."

Matthew decided it was time to speak up.

"Doctor, I have an idea," he said as he entered the room. "Please give me chance."

"I know that you and Jennifer were close," replied the doctor, "but there's nothing more that can be done. If you have any ideas, she's all yours."

Matthew pulled out his portable transfer unit, powered it on and aimed it at Jennifer.

"Abby, you there? I'm going to transmit a patient to you."

"Ready for receipt."

Matthew pulled the trigger, and Jennifer started to disappear. Within a few seconds, she was gone. The switch on the trigger worked like that of a gas pump—it automatically disengaged once the transfer was complete.

The nurse screamed. The attending doctor turned to Matthew and in a stern voice exclaimed, "Where did she go? What have you done with the body?"

"Don't worry," replied Matthew. "She's well in hand."

Matthew spoke into the microphone on the portable unit. "Abby, how long for repair?"

The voice over the speaker replied, "The patient has considerable physical damage and has lost 25 percent of her brain function due to oxygen starvation and physical trauma."

"Can you repair her? In fact, can you make her better than she was?"

There was a short pause, and then Abby came back with a response.

"Affirmative. Time for repair will be fifteen minutes twelve seconds. Enhancements will include increased brain function and physical endurance. An additional problem was found and will also be repaired."

"What was the problem?"

"Ovarian cancer."

"Very good, Abby. Let me know when you're ready for reassembly."

"Understood."

Matthew looked at the bewildered people in the room. Realizing that it would be best to say something to calm them down, he said, "Looks like we wait for the next fifteen minutes. After that, Jennifer should be back alive and in one piece."

"How's that possible?" asked the attending physician, whose name was Dr. James.

"How much do you know about my recent history?" asked Matthew.

"Not much, other than you were one of the lucky few that survived a lightning strike."

"While I was still in the hospital, the brain scan revealed some tremendous brain activity, which Dr. Gomez found truly astounding. Shortly after the accident, I discovered that I didn't need to sleep and that I could read and retain information like never before. During certain traumatic or stressful situations that I can't fully narrow down, my mind races and I can come up with solutions to problems that no one could even have conceived. During one of these episodes, I came up with this invention—an invention that can physically repair people."

"If that is really the case, you'll be a very famous man," said Dr. James. "The possibilities for a machine like that would be almost endless."

They spoke for another few minutes, and then the voice over the portable unit speaker interrupted them by saying, "Repair complete. Transmission and reassembly beginning."

Instantly, a figure started to reappear on the hospital bed. Within fifteen seconds, Jennifer had been fully reassembled. She opened her eyes, looked at Matthew and smiled. "Well, it took you long enough to get here."

Jennifer and Matthew laughed while the doctors and nurses just stared in amazement. After the bystanders recovered from their initial shock, they all started laughing to the point where tears streamed down their faces.

At length, Dr. James spoke up. "We'll leave you two alone for a few minutes, but I'd really like you to have a meeting with the hospital administrator and the hospital staff so that you can tell them about this invention of yours."

After the attending physician and nurses left, Matthew and Jennifer just looked at each other for a couple of minutes. Finally, Matthew smiled and said, "Abby did a pretty good job fixing your hair. It looks beautiful."

"I feel wonderful. In fact, I've never felt this good. I used to have a pain in my abdomen, but it's completely gone."

"Abby told me about the cancer you had. I believe you're feeling the result of her handiwork."

Jennifer got up, put her arms around Matthew's neck and gave him the biggest kiss he ever received. Not one to turn down a gift like that, he reciprocated, and they stayed in an embrace for several minutes.

"I'll tell you a little secret," he said after a few moments had passed. "I had some prayer time and the Lord told me that we would eventually get married."

Jennifer looked at Matthew and sarcastically replied, "I don't think we needed God to tell us that one!"

Matthew got so close to Jennifer that their noses touched. "But He also told me that we will have a daughter that will be great in the sight of the Lord. She will be powerful and a technological wiz. The Lord said it would have something to do with the combination of my altered genes and your altered chemistry after Abby fixed you up."

After a moment, Matthew kissed her nose. "I have to admit, you do look beautiful."

"How can you tell? You're only a millimeter away from me. All you can see are my eyes!"

They both laughed and then left the ICU hand in hand, with Matthew still carrying the portable unit. Dr. Butler met them outside. "Dr. Carpenter, I've set up a meeting with several doctors, nurses and the hospital management for 10 A.M. tomorrow morning. Can you be ready to give a presentation at that time?"

"I believe I can."

"Good. Now why don't the two of you get out of here, and we'll see you tomorrow."

"Sounds like a plan."

After Matthew and Jennifer had dinner, he took her back to her apartment, as she was now without a car. When they arrived, Matthew opened the door and helped her out of the car, and the two embraced.

"I sure wish I could come up with a way to enhance the invention so that it could be used more than once on a person," Matthew said as he held on to Jennifer. Once again, his mind started to race. She could feel the activity, and then they both felt the presence of God. "Children," a voice seemed to be saying, "though you are trying to do a noble thing, man was not meant to live forever in human form with flesh and blood."

"We understand, Lord," said Matthew. "What would You have us do then?"

"You are to use the machine for the good of mankind and to spread the gospel as often as you can. Your children will be My instruments for many years to come, and through the works of one of them, many people will be drawn to Me."

"We understand, Lord."

At that, the presence of the Lord left them.

"That was incredible," said Jennifer. "I've never felt the presence of the Lord in that way before."

After a few minutes, Matthew looked at Jennifer and said, "Because the Lord said that we'll have children—that is…in the plural—and a lot of other work to do, I guess we should think about getting started. So…I guess I should make this formal. Will you marry me?"

Jennifer looked at him with her head cocked to one side and tapped her right foot. "I'll need to think this over for a while." Then she grabbed him and blurted out, "I've thought long enough!" She then gave him a whopping big kiss.

"Does that mean 'Yes'?" said Matthew.

Jennifer just smiled.

Chapter 6

The Next Few Months

Matthew went home and spent the rest of the night working on some presentation slides for the briefing. The next morning he picked up Jennifer, and they had breakfast at a local restaurant. While eating, Matthew spoke up.

"I expect that this will go very well."

Jennifer looked at him skeptically. "I've got my fingers crossed."

Once they were done eating, they finished driving to the hospital and got there at about nine forty-five, where they were met by the chief surgeon and the hospital administrator. The hospital didn't have an auditorium, only a boardroom with enough room to seat about twenty people. Matthew decided to set up his laptop and projector in as convenient a location as possible for maximum visibility. People started coming in about nine fifty-five, and the room was jam-packed within minutes. The hospital administrator stood up to make the introduction.

"Good morning, everyone. I'm glad all of you could make it here for this presentation. Though Dr. Carpenter is very young, his fame is spreading rapidly. I myself know very little about his invention, but I have heard incredible things. Many of you already know Jennifer Tucker." Jennifer waved to the group, and the administrator continued.

"So without further ado, I introduce Dr. Matthew Carpenter." A round of applause filled the room for about fifteen seconds as Matthew got up.

"Thank you all for this invitation. I'll start by giving you a little history before I get into the reason for my being here. For those who don't know, I was on my way to my final graduation ceremony in the middle of a lightning storm with my now deceased wife, Sara, when she was killed. In terror and frustration, I got out of the car and was struck by lightning.

"Unlike the usual cases that end up with either major shock or cardiac arrest, my brain chemistry was altered so that I no longer need to sleep, am able to retain every detail of what I read, and can think as fast as a computer. I felt the urge to help people. When I heard of the recent hurricane, I immediately went to the disaster area to see what I could do. I was not at all prepared for what I would find.

"As I traveled through the destruction, I found a man and his eight-year-old daughter. She was in pretty bad shape—her leg was badly damaged and in need of amputation. I dropped her off at a hospital in South

Carolina and then got a flash in my mind about making this invention. After spending a couple of months building it and writing more than a million lines of software, it was about ready for a test."

"One evening recently, Jennifer and I witnessed a dog being run over by a car. I thought that the dog would make the perfect test case, as it was unlikely to live through the night. When the dog came back perfectly healthy, I knew that I had done something right." Matthew looked over at Jennifer and smiled.

"I figured that the next test was to actually attempt a rebuild of the little girl, named Anna. When that turned out successful, I brought her back to her home in South Carolina. Shortly thereafter, I learned that Jennifer had been in a car accident and was near death. She was in the hospital and I was unable to bring the machine I had invented to her, so I thought about a way to get the invention and her together. In the next twelve hours, I created a portable machine that could interface with my invention, which I call Abby. You can see the portable unit on the table next to Jennifer. I came to the hospital ICU just in time to witness Jennifer in cardiac arrest and see the portable unit work for the first time."

Matthew took a deep breath. "So much for a brief history."

Everyone in the room laughed.

"The basic principle of the invention," Matthew continued, "is manipulating cells independently so that the bad ones can be eliminated and the good ones can multiply at a rapid rate. Thus, through rapid cell multiplication and alteration, it is possible to rapidly replace unhealthy or missing pieces of the body. Although it takes a little bit longer to use the portable unit than the primary one due to having to transmit the entire body to a remote destination, the process is still very fast. To give you an idea on the time required for repair, the dog took two-and-a-half minutes, while Jennifer took about fifteen minutes."

"There is one drawback. Since there is some slight cell alteration, you cannot use the machine on a person more than once. Just as in organ replacement, sometimes the body will reject the cells and build up a resistance to the invader. In this case, we can fool the body once into accepting everything perfectly the first time, but we can't fool it twice—the absolute best we could do in that situation would be to just eliminate the bad cells. The problem, of course, would be that we couldn't replace the cells with anything, since the body would now be on the lookout for suspicious cells."

Just then a nurse came into the room. "I'm sorry to disturb you, doctor," she said, "but there's just been a car accident and two people are in critical condition. We need two doctors in ER immediately."

Matthew looked at the people in the room. "If you all are game, I could show you firsthand what the machine will do."

They all agreed, and the group adjourned to the ER.

"Which patient is in the most critical state?" asked Matthew.

"The woman over here has a head injury and glass all over her face and in her eyes," said the nurse. "She appears to have multiple internal injuries and may have a collapsed lung. It's not likely that she'll make it much longer."

Matthew turned on the portable unit and aimed it at the lady, who appeared to be in her forties.

"Abby, prepare for transmission."

A voice over the portable unit intercom said, "Ready for disassembly and transmission."

Matthew pulled the trigger and immediately the lady began to disappear. Within ten seconds she was completely gone. Everyone in the room just gasped with amazement.

"Time for repair: five minutes thirteen seconds," came the voice over the portable unit speaker.

"I'm afraid that I can't do more than one at a time," said Matthew, "so we should make sure the other patient is stable."

"Though his injuries are extensive, he is at least stable," said the nurse.

"Good. Does anyone have any basic questions that I can answer while we're waiting?"

A nurse in her early thirties spoke up first. "I'm guessing that you haven't had time to do any studies of the long-term effects on patients."

"Quite right. So far, we've managed to only experiment on patients that are terminal…or in Jennifer's case, are already dead. In a sense, we used cases that were already beyond anything that medical science could do—and thus, nobody had anything to lose."

The voice could once again be heard over the portable unit speaker. "Repair complete. Beginning reassembly and transmission."

As the doctors and nurses in the room watched in disbelief, the woman began to reappear. Although she looked a little disoriented, she seemed to now be in perfect health.

"Jennifer, please see how she is while we work on the next one."

"You got it."

Matthew thought for a second and then spoke up. "This will be the first patient that has not been diagnosed as terminal, although his injuries are extensive. Do I have the approval from the hospital to perform the repair on this patient?"

The hospital administrator and attending physicians all agreed to the risk, and so Matthew continued with the next patient. Once Matthew and Abby completed the repair, both patients were found to be in perfect health.

"Well, shall we adjourn to the conference room to continue our discussion?" asked Matthew. They all agreed and worked their way back to the boardroom. The nurses and doctors were buzzing with chatter all the way back.

"So what do you all think is our way forward from here?" asked Matthew. "I'm willing to rent the unit to the hospital for $100.00 per use. This will help pay for my building cost while at the same time making it affordable for everyone. I can also build more units. If you want more business than you can handle, I'll allow this hospital to be the main distribution point for all services provided. You just need to remember that it's a one shot deal—and patients need to know that as well.

The machine does not make you immortal, but it can extend your life for a season. One other point: Please don't charge exorbitant prices for the use of the machine. I would also like the ability to build a unit for myself as a testing ground for new features."

The hospital administrator stood up and addressed both Matthew and the rest of the crowd. "What you have done is truly amazing. We'll gladly accept your offer of being the exclusive distributor of services and paying you per service. We'll also decide when best to offer this service due to its being, as you say, a 'one shot deal.' We'll get a room ready for the equipment immediately and have someone work with you to get it here. We'll also set up a training class for tomorrow at 10 A.M."

The hospital administrator began clapping, and the entire assembly soon followed. They continued clapping and whistling for at least a minute. Matthew took a quick bow and stretched out his hand to Jennifer, who decided to curtsy.

Matthew and Jennifer left and spent the rest of the day getting Abby ready to go to her new home. Early the next day, the movers arrived and managed to get Abby safely installed in the hospital by nine A.M. Matthew gave the first training class an hour later. There were lots of questions, as all present were eager to learn about the new system and its possibilities.

One question of particular interest to the audience was brought up by one of the technicians: "How do you know what sort of questions to ask the computer?"

"The best thing to do is to start with an analysis," replied Matthew. "Once the analysis is complete, you can lead Abby to perform the desired act. It may be as simple as asking her to perform the repair or, in some cases of ambiguity, asking a few additional questions that would eliminate any possible guessing."

"You mean like asking a child what hurts, leading to possible conclusions?"

"You could think of it that way. Most circumstances will be pretty straightforward. If all else fails, you can ask one of the doctors for advice or call me. I'll go ahead and put my home and cell numbers on the machine, just in case. Something to keep in mind is that you can always ask Abby for advice. I programmed her with some good detective skills, and she will normally come to pretty decent conclusions on her own."

The staff searched the hospital for willing patients who were gravely or terminally ill, and then each student was given the chance to try his or her hand at a repair while the others watched. This allowed for all participants to see Abby in action and witness variations in procedure. When all the students had been trained, Matthew and Jennifer looked at each other, smiled and gave a big sigh of relief.

News traveled fast. Matthew was asked to give another demonstration the next day at the same time for other area hospital administrators. What he saw when he arrived nearly took his breath away—news crews, big wigs from the government, the Surgeon General and numerous other people of high standing within the medical community had all shown up to witness the demonstration.

In fact, by the time Matthew arrived there that day, the machine had already been used more than fifty times. All the people that had used the machine—including the technicians, nurses and doctors—were quite pleased with themselves for picking it up so quickly.

"Well, that's over $5,000," Matthew said to himself. "That should pay for some of the materials I spent on Abby."

The new demonstration went so well that Matthew received orders for thirty more primary units and an additional sixty portable units. With the number of orders received, Matthew decided that it was time to contact Jonathan and SIMUTECKNIK for assistance. So the next day he e-mailed the list of parts to SIMUTECK-NIK, and within a week he was down at the company giving a course on how to assemble the units and load the software.

Matthew gave individual names to each of the machines. To come up with the names, he decided to use the same concept as naming hurricanes and just go down the alphabet. He always used girls' names, as the three most influential people in his life were girls—namely Sara, Anna and Jennifer.

Once Matthew finished with the assembly training, he and Jennifer went back home and started planning their wedding. He also started an interview and speaking tour, and Jennifer went with him on all his engagements to keep him out of trouble. Matthew even received the Nobel Prize for medicine that year. In spite of all this, he remained humble and continued giving credit for all his successes to the Lord.

Matthew and Jennifer were married four months after he received the Nobel Prize. By that time he had made close to $10 million in royalties, and the money kept rolling in. Their wedding was a truly beautiful one. Jennifer looked incredible in her wedding dress, as did Matthew in his tuxedo—although he felt a bit awkward, as he had never worn a tux in his life.

When the wedding was over and Matthew and Jennifer were dancing their final dance at the reception, Matthew couldn't resist whispering something in her ear, though he was chuckling as he did it. "You know, every time I look at you, I can't help but think how marvelous a job Abby did on you. I couldn't have done better myself."

They burst out laughing so hard that the entire assembly turned to look at them. When someone asked Matthew what the joke was about, all he could say was, "We were just discussing an assembly issue," which made both of them laugh all the more.

Chapter 7

Good News

"Honey, I think I'm pregnant," Jennifer said one day.

Matthew looked up and smiled. "What do you want to name her?"

"How do you know it's a 'her'?"

"That's what the Lord said."

"All the Lord said was that we would have a girl and that she was going to be great. He didn't say which child she would be."

Matthew thought for a moment about this. "You know, you're pretty smart. I hadn't given that a thought. Must be that extra brain power I had Abby give to you."

They both laughed, and then Matthew spoke up again.

"Jen, what do you suppose we should focus on next for a new invention?"

"I've been thinking about that, and what I came up with was a way to help infertile couples without having to use up their 'one shot.' After all, it would be a shame for couples to have to use the machine for a relatively simple fertility problem."

"That's an excellent idea, my lovely pregnant wife."

Matthew started thinking and suddenly found that his mind was racing. Jennifer could see it happening. She got closer to him and could feel the energy. It felt almost like a large electromagnetic field. After a few minutes Matthew opened his eyes and said, "Of course, there's no reason why it couldn't work."

"What is it? What did you come up with?"

"Actually, it's a simple adjustment to the machine that we already have. I just have to limit the scope of the repair to the damaged organs. We'll play a little game with the cells to make them think that they're not being invaded. This should work for those cases in which we are not doing any major repairs."

Matthew went right to work on the modifications to the software. Forty-seven hours later, Matthew came up to Jennifer, put his arms around her and said, "OK, Hon, do you know anyone you'd like to try this out on?"

"As a matter of fact, I do. One of my college girl-friends has been trying to get pregnant for the past five years. The doctors don't know what the problem is."

"Well, why don't you call them and invite them over?"

"I already have. They're just waiting for my confirmation call to be here within the hour."

"Wow. You're good!"

Jennifer called her girlfriend, and an hour later there was a knock at the door. Both Matthew and Jennifer went to answer it. Matthew saw a woman about Jennifer's age about 5'7" tall with long brown hair and blue eyes. She was accompanied by a man about the same age who was about six feet tall. They came in and greeted Jennifer and Matthew with a hearty handshake. The look in their eyes and on their faces was one of hope. Jennifer spoke up first.

"Hi Betty, I'm guessing this is your husband, Roger."

"That's me," said Roger with a hearty laugh.

"Come on in and sit down while Matthew asks you a few questions."

They all went in the living room and Jennifer had their guests sit together on one of the couches. The hosts sat on two chairs facing them.

"What have the doctors you have seen done for you?" asked Matthew.

"We've gone through every test imaginable," said Betty.

"Well, that narrows it down," Matthew said with a smile. "OK, we'll take the brute force approach and get you over to Ally."

"I thought your invention was named Abby?" asked Roger.

"The first one was, but that one went to the local hospital. I've made or subcontracted more than 300 at this point. The one I currently have is named Ally."

Matthew led Betty and Roger into the workshop while Jennifer took up the rear. "Go ahead and lie down on the table while I close the door," he said to Betty.

Betty lay down and Matthew powered up Ally. "Disassemble and analyze, paying specific attention to reproductive functions," he said to the machine.

"Acknowledged."

In a flash, Betty was gone. After a few seconds, Ally came back with a response. "Analysis complete. Patient is within normal parameters for all reproductive functions."

Matthew thought for a few seconds. "Keep within memory the patient's entire chemical analysis and then reassemble."

"Acknowledged."

Almost instantly, Betty reappeared.

"Now it's your turn, Roger."

Roger traded places with Betty, giving her a kiss as they passed each other.

"Ally, disassemble and analyze again, paying specific attention to reproductive functions."

"Acknowledged."

Roger disappeared in a similar manner to Betty.

"Analysis complete. Patient is within normal parameters for all reproductive functions."

Matthew looked up at the ceiling in thought. "Ally, cross-correlate parameters between this patient and the previous patient and determine if there is any incompatibility."

"Acknowledged."

About thirty seconds later Ally came back with a response. "Analysis complete. Although both patients are within normal parameters, each are at the lowest end of the spectrum for all functions. This decreases their probability of success by two orders of magnitude."

Matthew thought for a moment and then spoke to Ally as the others watched with a high level of anticipation. "Alter the patient's reproductive organs to the highest end of the spectrum, thereby optimizing chances for fertilization. On completion, reassemble."

"Acknowledged."

After about twenty seconds, Roger reappeared and looked at the others rather inquisitively.

"Betty, you trade places with Roger again."

They swapped places and again gave each other a kiss.

"Ally, disassemble and alter the patient's reproductive organs to the highest end of the spectrum, thereby optimizing chances for fertilization, implantation, and ability to carry through to term with an optimal ease of birthing. On completion, reassemble."

"Acknowledged."

In a flash Betty was gone, and then reappeared in what seemed like only a few seconds. She opened her eyes and got off the table, not knowing what to do next.

"So what now, doc?" asked Roger.

"I think you should be OK. Go home, have fun, don't worry about any of this and just let us know when you are expecting." Roger and Betty looked at each other with hopeful looks while Matthew and Jennifer just looked at each other and smiled.

After dinner when their guests had left, Jennifer looked at Matthew with a rather inquisitive yet sarcastic look.

"Do you realize what we just did to Betty and Roger?"

"Yup."

"How many children do you think they'll have?"

Matthew shrugged his shoulders and replied, "Only God knows."

Jennifer shook her head from side to side and looked toward the ceiling. Seeing her, Matthew started chuckling, and then Jennifer followed suit.

Part 2

Starr Gazer

Chapter 8

The Early Years

"Give me one more little push and the head will be out," said Matthew softly.

"Easy for you to say," replied Jennifer. "Actually, this is much easier than what my mother told me."

"That's another one you can thank Abby for."

Jennifer looked at her husband with one eye open and her head cocked. She grunted, and the head was out.

"Give me another one and I think we can get the shoulders to come through. Then we'll be home free."

Jennifer looked at Matthew with one of those skeptical stares. She waited for the head to rotate and then pushed. The shoulders came out, followed by the rest of the body. Matthew immediately put the small body on Jenny's belly, and all three cried.

"Surprise, it's a girl!" said Jennifer. She and Matthew looked at each other, both well knowing what they were expecting, as the Lord led them to believe it would be a girl.

"She's really beautiful," said Jennifer. "But I think I'm just a little bit partial. Come on, Hon, help me count all the fingers and toes."

"OK, dear."

They proceeded to count all the fingers, toes, eyes, ears and anything else they could find.

"She really is gorgeous," said Matthew. He let the cord stop pulsating before he clamped and cut it.

"Let her go ahead and nurse a little so that we can have a few more contractions and get the placenta out."

The baby latched on immediately and the contractions kicked in right away. Within a few minutes the placenta was out. Matthew cleaned up while Jennifer bonded with the baby. She just couldn't take her eyes off the baby. "Look at how much hair she has. It's as blonde as mine. Do you think it'll stay that way?"

"Hard to tell. Some babies' hair is blonde at birth but then changes later. Others stay blonde."

After another few minutes, Jennifer spoke again. "I'm sure glad we did this at home. I feel so much more comfortable here."

"Well…you were low risk and everything looked fine. No reason not to have the baby here. By the way, we never did decide what to name her."

"If she is going to be as famous as God said, then we need to come up with a good name. She's a good sucker, but somehow I don't think that would work." That comment kept them laughing for a whole minute.

"OK, let's both close our eyes for a minute, hold hands, pray and see what the Lord leads us to name her," said Matthew. They closed their eyes and then both blurted out at the same time, "Starr!"

Jennifer looked at the baby and then at Matthew. "You do realize that there's some significance to that name."

"Somehow I figured that one out all by myself."

"I don't suppose we'll know for a while, right?"

"I'm pretty good at some things, but I expect that's one that God is keeping to Himself."

During the next few months, Matthew and Jennifer were surprised to see how alert the baby was and how she seemed to know exactly what they were doing. Jennifer and Matthew decided to read to the baby every chance they could get. It appeared as if the baby followed along with everything they did. By the time Starr was six months old, they decided to also start reading math and science books to her. It was truly amazing to see how the baby could absorb the material like a sponge.

By age two, Starr was reading books on her own. She had a photographic memory and seemed to be requiring less and less sleep every day. Although most normal children require eight to ten hours of sleep each night, Starr didn't seem to need more than three hours.

"Honey, I can't stay up as long as this child. Tell you what, since you don't need any sleep, you take the night watch and I'll take the day watch."

"That sounds fair enough."

"That should give you a lot of time to spend with her. You can probably teach her a lot of the things that you already know."

"I can do that, but at her rate of learning it won't be long before she'll be way past me."

By age five, Starr was reading at the college level and could do differential equations in her head. Advanced calculus was mere child's play—which seemed quite amusing, since she was still a pretty small child.

"I think we've come to a crossroads," Matthew said to Jennifer one day. "Starr is advancing faster than we can keep up."

"Honey, I really think we need to get her around other children so that she can grow up as a normal child. Besides, I think I'm pregnant again, which means I won't quite have as much time to devote to Starr as I have been."

"Why didn't you tell me you were pregnant?"

"I just figured it out today for myself. It's not like I've known for weeks."

Matthew went and gave Jennifer a hug, and then got back to business.

"In any case, she'll never be a normal child," Matthew said with a smile. "Remember, she takes after me."

Jennifer burst out laughing. "You got that one right."

Matthew continued, "I do think you're right about the socialization aspects, though."

"Isn't there a Christian School not too far away from here?"

"Yes, Waynesport Christian School. It's just about a mile away."

"How about if I give them a call?"

"Sure. It sounds like a good idea."

About a half hour later, Jennifer came over to Matthew and Starr. "I just got off the phone with the principal at Waynesport," she said. "He's got time to see us in a few minutes if we can get over there. So…get your shoes on. We're going for a little ride."

They arrived at the school about fifteen minutes later. The outside of the school looked nice enough. It was a two story brick building divided into two sections. One side said "Waynesport Christian Elementary School" and the other said "Waynesport Christian High School." The family walked into the elementary school and stopped at an office near the entrance. There, they were told that the principal's office was down the hall on the left.

They knocked on the door of the principal's office and were told to come right in. The principal stood up from his chair, shook their hands and introduced himself.

"Hello. I'm David Myerhuff, the elementary school principal."

"I'm Dr. Matthew Carpenter, this is my wife, Jennifer, and this is our daughter, Starr."

"How do you do," David said with a smile.

Matthew spoke up next. "How much do you know about me?"

"I know that you're a famous doctor. I don't know many details."

"Well, let me tell you a little about myself. I was struck by lightning about six years ago and now I can read and retain everything with a photographic memory. I don't need to sleep, and I can invent some very extraordinary things. When Jennifer and I were married and Starr was born, she inherited many of my abilities. In fact, it seems as if she even has more abilities than I have."

"We'd like you to treat Starr like any other student," said Jennifer. "She's already smarter than Matthew and me combined. We've enrolled her in night classes at the University so that she can get a degree. She has an aptitude for biochemistry and nuclear physics."

The principal was taken aback. "I'm not sure we can handle this," he replied.

"We've told Starr to play and interact with other children her own age. We want her to know what other children are like," Matthew explained.

"We'll give it our best shot. We've never had a student smarter than we were. Let me get Miss Gloria Temple, the teacher who would be assigned to Starr. We'll be starting school in another week so she is here getting prepared."

David pressed an intercom button on his desk and spoke into the microphone. "Miss Temple, please report to the principal's office. Miss Temple, to the principal's office."

About a minute later, a girl in her mid-twenties wearing glasses and with shoulder length chestnut brown hair walked into the room. When David saw her, he spoke up.

"Miss Temple, this is Matthew and Jennifer Carpenter and their daughter, Starr."

"Hello, Dr. Carpenter. I've heard a lot about your invention. You're pretty famous in my family. Abby saved my father's life."

"Glad to be of service."

Once the pleasantries were finished, David spoke up again.

"Starr will be one of your students next week."

Gloria looked at Starr with a big smile. "Hello Starr. How about if I show you where our classroom is?"

"That would be wonderful, Miss Temple," said Starr.

Gloria held out her hand and Starr took it. As they were about to walk out the door, David spoke up.

"Miss Temple."

"Yes sir?"

"There is something else that you should know. The main reason for Starr being here is for socialization. She is already taking courses at the university. She's a wiz at calculus."

Miss Temple looked at the principal almost in shock and then down at Starr. After a few seconds, she spoke up. "I understand, sir. Come on, Starr. We've got some exploring to do."

"Yippee!" Starr replied with a big smile.

After they left the room, David and the parents looked at each other with sighs of relief.

By the time Starr was ten, she had Bachelor of Science degrees in biochemistry, nuclear physics, sociology and astronomy. By age twelve, she had received doctoral degrees in biochemistry and nuclear physics. She was only in the seventh grade at the Waynesport Christian School, but she was a model student in everything she did. She was excellent in sports, a black belt in karate and the fastest runner in the state. By the time she was twelve, she didn't need to sleep at all.

On her thirteenth birthday, Starr had a party and invited a number of her school friends who were about the same age. She had turned into a very lovely girl, with long curly blonde hair down to her hips—good looks that came from her mother.

As evening approached, she went outside with her telescope and showed her friends what the different stars, constellations and nebula were. As she gazed up at the stars that cool brisk night, she wondered what it would be like to be able to harness the power of the stars. After the party was over and her mother and brother were asleep, she and her father sat down to talk.

"Dad?" she said.

"Yes, honey."

"I've been thinking. Wouldn't it be incredible to harness the power of stars and be able to use the power to help mankind?"

"Indeed it would. The power would be virtually limitless."

Starr sat next to her father and gave him a big hug. After a minute, she held his hand and looked in his eyes. Suddenly their hands started sparking, much like static electricity, although much more concentrated. What was interesting was that it didn't stop once their hands were clasped together. The two of them soon realized that they couldn't pull their hands apart, and as they gazed into each other's eyes, formulas and pictures started racing through their minds at incredible speed. There were designs for force fields, weapons, a special suit, a mode for invisibility, and numerous other designs as well. All in all, it took about an hour for everything to complete.

When their minds had returned to normal, Starr looked at her father with wide eyes and an expression of total shock on her face. Things like this had never happened to her before—only to her father.

"All I can say is, 'wow!'" said Matthew.

Once Starr had calmed down and her breathing was back to normal, she decided that it was her time to speak, though her voice was still a bit shaky.

"I guess I've got some work to do," she said. She looked at her father with a loving smile and then continued, "You up for giving me a hand?"

Matthew looked at her with a smirk and replied, "I thought you'd never ask."

Chapter 9

A Surprise Test

The two night owls spent the rest of the evening talking about their experience and comparing notes to see if each of them had experienced exactly the same thing. Once they realized that they had—to even the smallest detail—they decided it was time to act.

"Let's identify all the tasks and then divide them up between the two of us," said Starr. "There's capturing the power; building the suit; allowing for flight capability; getting to hypersonic speeds; interfacing with Ally; generating a force field, weapon systems, sensor systems, cloaking devices, tracking systems and countermeasures; figuring out the ability to time warp; writing all the related software; and working out how the system is activated and how the suit is transmitted to the user."

"Not exactly a small job is it?"

"There are a couple more things that are almost as hard."

"What's that?"

"A name for the superhero and some way to activate it."

"We'll, here's a few names I can think of: Super Starr, Wonder Girl, IncrediStarr."

Starr looked at her father with her eyebrows raised. "I really don't think so."

"Well....how about Starr Gazer?"

"Hey, that sounds like a cool name. It's got a double meaning. OK, so how do we activate it? I always liked the different ways that cartoon characters used to activate their powers. You know, like, '*Dwarf stars of the galaxy, black holes of the universe, lend me your powers...NOW!* Or maybe, '*By the power of the Dwarf Star!*'"

"You should probably choose something that doesn't take so long to say, since you don't know what sort of circumstances you will be in when you would need to use it."

"I think you have a good point, Dad."

Matthew thought for a couple of minutes and then spoke up. "How about something like, '*Starr power...activate!*'"?

"That's pretty catchy, Dad. I like it."

By that time the rest of the family was awake. As Matthew served breakfast, he and Starr explained to the rest of the family what had happened while they slept.

"And I thought our life would be boring from this point forward," said Jennifer as she smiled and shook her head from side to side.

"Wait until I tell all the kids at school that my sister is going to be a superhero!" exclaimed Andrew.

"Hold on there, Son," replied Matthew with a very stern look. "We don't have anything built and we don't even know if it'll work."

"Your father is right," noted Jennifer. "At least on the part about nothing being built." After a few seconds she added, "I'm sure that if your father has given it some thought, it'll likely work. Nevertheless, you need to be quiet about this until all the tests have been completed." With her head down and a very stern motherly look she added, "Do you understand, Andrew?"

Andrew knew that her mother meant it when she called him "Andrew." Usually she called him "Andy" or "honey." He decided it was best to answer in the affirmative.

"Yes, mother."

Matthew and Starr spent the next five months working on the project and conducting various simple tests along the way. Matthew wrote the majority of the software and the interface to Ally, as those were the areas with which he was the most familiar. He implanted a device into Starr that would act as the activation device and also as a failsafe device in case of an emergency. With this device in place, all Starr would have to do was say the special phrase and an influx of equipment would suit her up. It was very late one Thursday night in April, about five A.M., when they finally completed the project.

"OK, my number one daughter, we'll try this out after you get back from school today."

"Aw, Dad. Can't we try it out now? I've memorized all the ways to activate the weapons, sensors, and other various modes."

"With all this equipment, we're going to need some time to test everything out. This is extremely complex. If one piece of equipment fails you're up the creek. Besides, you'll need to get used to it before you are involved in some major crisis."

"OK, I guess you're right." She gave him a big hug, and he gave her a kiss on the forehead. "I love you, Dad."

"I love you too, honey. You and I can relate to each other unlike anyone else on this planet."

The next day started like any other. Jennifer could smell the aroma of pancakes and homemade sausage and knew that Starr must have been experimenting again. Most things that Starr prepared for meals were very tasty, even if they had never been attempted before. Jennifer quickly dressed and noticed that Andrew was just getting ready to walk out of his room. They both entered the kitchen and saw that Starr had a big plate of sausage patties and flapjacks already waiting for them. She gave her mother and brother a hug.

"Boy, that smells good," said Jennifer. "You must have been working on that for an hour already."

"Almost. It's already seven A.M. and I need to be at school by seven forty-five. If I jog fast, I can get there in about seven minutes."

Jennifer went over and tasted a piece of sausage. "Mmm, I've never had sausage that tasted this good. What in the world did you do to it?"

"I threw in a little salt, pepper, sage, coriander, red pepper and a little maple syrup."

"I've done that before, but mine doesn't normally come out this well."

Starr smiled and said, "I must have a special touch."

Just before she left for school, Matthew came in from the workshop and spoke to her. "We'll see if we can run a few experiments tonight, and maybe in a few days we'll be ready for a real trial."

"OK, Dad." She gave him a big hug and started thinking about the day ahead of her. At seven thirty, she ran out the door with her school supplies in her backpack and started a slow jog to school.

Starr's last class before lunch was geometry. It happened to be the farthest from the cafeteria, and she was always one of the last children to get in the cafeteria line, as she liked talking to Mr. Tibbs, her teacher. Mr. Tibbs never minded talking to Starr because she always had some new way of looking at the subject. On this day as they were discussing one particularly interesting problem with proofs, they suddenly heard four gunshots from down the hall. They both froze for a second, and then Starr decided to find out what happened.

She ran out of the classroom and headed in the direction where she thought the noise had come from. When she came across some other children screaming and running in the opposite direction, she knew that she was headed to the right place—the cafeteria. She slowly worked her way with through and finally arrived at the cafeteria doors. Bursting into the room, she went about ten feet and then suddenly stopped. There she saw her best friend, Cindy, lying on the floor in a pool of blood with another friend, Julie, next to her.

There were two boys with pistols in their hands about fifteen feet from the bodies. They were laughing and swinging the guns around as if they were quite pleased with themselves. These were the Tyler twins, and they tended to have a mean streak in them. Their parents had recently gone through a divorce, and the children had pretty much been ignored during the whole process. When the boys saw Starr come in, they turned toward her.

Jimmy spoke up. "Well, if it isn't Miss Smarty Pants. Think you're cool, huh? You're going to be dead in a few minutes. Got anything to say?"

Starr started thinking about all the things she could say but soon realized that the only hope she had was to activate her new untested suit. She knew that this was also the only chance that her friends had of coming out of the situation alive. She had to quickly disarm the boys and get the girls to Ally so that it could repair them.

Starr stood perfectly still, closed her eyes, took a deep breath and spoke in a loud voice, "Starr power...activate!" Instantly an immense light flashed all around, and

Starr felt the suit being put over her. Once the process was complete, she said, "Activate force field!"

The boys were completely caught by surprise, as was everyone else in the room. A few other boys who were squatting behind some chairs looked back and forth between the twins and Starr, just staring with their mouths wide open.

It didn't take too long for the twins to realize that they might be in trouble. With the four shots they each had left, the boys opened fire on Starr and didn't let up until the guns were empty. When they realized that the bullets had no effect on her whatsoever, they started to panic and become desperate.

Starr took this opportunity to put a stop to the mayhem. She raised her right hand and said, "Set weapons to heavy stun." A second later, flashes of light like laser beams came out of her hand and pushed the boys about twenty feet to the opposite wall. Their guns fell from their hands, and they fell down unconscious.

Starr immediately went over to Cindy and Julie to access their wounds. Julie was still alive, but it seemed that Cindy was not. "Ally, prepare for emergency patient transport," Starr said into her intercom.

"Understood," came the reply over the speaker.

"Ally, transport, analyze, and repair."

"Acknowledged."

Starr placed her hands on Cindy, and within a few seconds her friend had disappeared. The boys hiding behind the chairs in the back of the room didn't know what to do. They didn't know whether to run out of the room, tie up the Tyler boys, or help Starr. In the end they just stayed crouched where they were with their mouths wide open.

"Ally, what's the report?" said Starr.

"Patient is severely brain damaged," said the voice over the speaker. "She was shot both in the forehead and also in the chest area. Her heart has been blown apart and her left lung is totally collapsed."

"Can you repair her?"

"Patient was dead for more than three minutes. Full integrity cannot be guaranteed."

"Dad, are you there?"

"Yes, honey. What happened?"

"Cindy and Julie were shot by the Tyler twins. Ally isn't sure if Cindy will pull through. Is there anything that you can do?"

Matthew took control of Ally. "Ally, repair all functions that you can guarantee."

"Understood."

A few minutes later, Ally came back with a response. "Repairs complete on all but the brain functions."

"Ally, what would it take to repair the brain functions?" said Matthew.

"Approximately 35.2 petawatts."

"Holy guacamole! Starr, can you transmit 35.2 petawatts to Ally?"

"I think so," replied Starr. "Dad, you realize that we've never tried anything like this before?"

"We're doing lots of firsts today, honey. So…you about ready?"

Starr set a few parameters on her suit to transmit the power and then spoke over the intercom. "Ally, prepare to receive the power you need to fix the patient."

"Acknowledged."

"Transmitting."

In the distance, Starr could hear sirens. She knew that she had to hurry. A minute later, Ally came back with a response. "Repair complete. Transmission to Starr Gazer proceeding."

Within seconds, Cindy appeared in front of Starr, quite bewildered but very healthy. Starr walked over to Julie and checked her vitals. She was unconscious, but still breathing.

"Ally, prepare to receive the next patient."

"Acknowledged."

Julie disappeared. After a few moments had passed, Starr asked Ally what the extent of the repairs would be.

"Patient was shot both in the small intestine and in the right lung areas," came the reply. "Repair will take three minutes forty-seven seconds."

Starr looked over at Cindy, who still seemed to be in shock. "It's OK, Cindy. It's me, Starr. I rendered the Tyler twins powerless for a while and helped my father's machine, Ally, put you back together. That was a close one. We almost lost you. Ally's working on Julie right now."

"Oh, Starr!" cried Cindy. "It was absolutely terrible. The Tyler boys came into the lunchroom and started making jokes about the school and all the teachers. Julie and I tried to make them stop—and that's when they pulled out the pistols. They started shooting. I don't remember anything after the first shot."

"I'm not surprised that you don't remember much, considering there wasn't much of you left to do any remembering." They hugged each other until a voice over the speaker said, "Ready to transmit patient."

Within seconds, Julie appeared within a few feet of Starr and Cindy. With a sigh of relief, Starr said, "Starr power…deactivate." Instantly there was a bright flash of light. Once it diminished, Starr was again in her regular school clothes.

The three girls hugged each other as the sound from the police sirens grew louder and then abruptly stopped. About fifteen seconds later, the police entered the cafeteria. They went over to the boys, handcuffed them, woke them up and then read them their rights. They picked up the guns as evidence. A detective came over to interview all the girls.

After the police dragged off the boys, the principal came in and gave all the girls a hug. "Well, I suppose it would be best if I dismissed school a little early today. Although I see that you are all OK, it's been a most traumatic day."

Starr winked at Cindy and Julie, and all three of them smiled at each other.

How the Government Became Involved

News about Matthew and Starr traveled fast and reporters were soon continually badgering them for interviews. Not only were Matthew and Starr receiving calls from the major networks and all the famous interview shows, but they were also receiving requests from journalists and regular hometown reporters who were waiting for the one story that would provide them their break into the big time.

As Matthew was about to hang up on one particularly insistent reporter, the reporter broke in one last time and said, "Why won't you talk to me? This is big news. The public deserves to know about this!"

Matthew knew that he had to say something. What did this reporter know about the public? How many lives had he saved? Matthew decided it was high time to give him a piece of his mind, though it went against his better judgment.

"The only reason you want me to talk to you is for your own benefit...so you can get that big scoop that will propel your career. It has nothing to do with the public interest. You claim that the public deserves to know, but I tell you that it has no need to know. Any time that heroes are placed in the public eye, it generally brings their downfall. If you were truly interested in helping the public, you would do the opposite of what you are doing. To you this is just a business, but to the people involved it's their lives that are being affected."

There was a short pause, and then Matthew continued. "What sort of questions would you ask, anyway? How much power Starr has? What type of things she can do? What are the limits of her abilities? If we answered these questions, we would be giving some enemy a way to find a weakness to exploit. How would you feel if a weakness that you helped to reveal were to be exploited at a time when she could have saved you or one of your loved ones? Your exposing a weakness could mean your own death."

There was silence on the other end of the phone for a few seconds, and then the reporter spoke up.

"I never thought about it like that. How about if I come up with a list of questions that would be more of a human-interest or community-oriented story and send them to you? Maybe you can answer any of those that you feel are appropriate and then get back to me. That way, I'll get something without placing you in an awkward position. I'll also make sure you are not misquoted."

Matthew seemed pleased with this idea. "That's the fairest response I've heard out of any reporter. OK, you've got a deal. Oh, by the way, this will work two ways. If you do a good job, you'll continue to get the exclusive story every time something happens. But if you blow it…you won't get anything ever again."

The reporter seemed pleased at possibly being the exclusive reporter for this big ongoing story. He responded rather excitedly to Matthew's proposal, and the two ended their conversation.

After the detective interviewed Starr at school, she didn't hear anything else about the case for a couple weeks. Then one day after Starr got home from school, there was a knock at the door. When Jennifer opened it, there were two gentlemen standing there. They were very neatly dressed. Each had a dark two-piece suit and short hair. As they pulled out their badges, Jennifer saw that each of them carried a gun under their suit coats. The one man with glasses spoke up first.

"Good afternoon, ma'am. I'm detective Michael Taylor, and this is Federal Agent Daniel Thompson. We're not really here on official business, but we would appreciate it if we could talk to Matthew and Starr for a few minutes."

Jennifer realized that there was nothing to fear from these two gentlemen, so she didn't mind granting their request. "That would be fine," she said. "Come on in while I get them."

Jennifer turned around and called out into the house in a loud voice, "Starr! Matthew! You've got some visitors." About ten seconds later, Matthew and Starr came in the room. Detective Taylor spoke up before Jennifer could even attempt to make the introductions.

"How do you do? I'm detective Michael Taylor, and this is Federal Agent Daniel Thompson."

All parties shook hands and then detective Taylor spoke again. "Starr, you may remember me from when I interviewed you at school."

"Yes, of course. Nice to see you again, sir." Although the two officers seemed very professional and polite, Jennifer could see from their mannerisms that they had an agenda.

"If you remember," continued detective Taylor, "I had only managed to get to the school after all the events of the day had taken place. Although I heard about all that happened, it seemed difficult for me to believe that a thirteen-year-old girl would be able to overpower two boys with guns and then bring a girl back to life who had been blown to pieces."

"Both Michael and I are very dedicated to serving our community and nation," interrupted agent Thompson. "We want to do what is best to keep everyone safe, and we would like to have the best resources we can in fighting crime."

At this point, Matthew, Starr and Jennifer could clearly tell by the way the law enforcement officers were fidgeting and swallowing that they were getting a little more nervous. After Agent Thompson swallowed one more time, he seemed to get up enough courage to continue speaking.

"We know of Dr. Carpenter's fame with the healing machines and of Starr's incredible knowledge. We were hoping that you'd allow us to call you with any difficult cases that we have from time to time and, if you were willing, perhaps help us solve them."

Matthew and Starr looked at each other and nodded. "Actually, we created these inventions for the good of mankind," said Matthew. "We'd be honored to help…though we do have a couple of requests."

"Go ahead," said detective Taylor after a few seconds of silence between the parties had passed.

"We would really be honored to help our community, nation and world…but we would really like to be kept out of the limelight as much as possible. The last thing we want is to have our work impeded by politics and journalists."

The two agents breathed a sigh of relief once they realized that the conditions were quite fair. The two men began to smile. After another few seconds, Agent Thompson decided it was time to speak up.

"Those sound like fair requests. We will make sure that you get whatever tools you think are necessary and that you're adequately compensated. We can come up with some way to put you people on a payroll as subcontractors."

Matthew thought for a moment. "I'll tell you what," he said. "Let's go for a drive out to a little deserted area out Robinson Road. We'll give you a quick demonstration of Starr's special suit to give you a feel of what it can do. We created it as a sort of prototype unit. Once we get all the kinks worked out—and if everything goes well—we will need some guidance as to how to distribute these units to benefit the whole world. As you might expect, we are going to have to be much more selective in distributing these units than we were with the previous invention."

The officers agreed with this idea and soon the detective, the agent, Matthew and Starr all left the house and climbed into Matthew's new SUV. Matthew drove the group out to the deserted site, an old gravel pit. There were old pieces of machinery there. They all got out of the car, and Matthew looked at Starr. "OK, Starr. The show's all yours."

Starr walked about twenty feet away and spoke her now famous words, "Starr power...activate!"

There was an immense flash of light that was so bright that Matthew and the officers had to shield their eyes. Once the light dissipated, the officers saw that Starr was now dressed in a uniform with numerous gadgets attached.

"Enable invisibility mode," said Starr. With that, she disappeared. The law enforcement officials' jaws dropped.

In a few seconds, Starr reappeared in a different spot. "Enable flight mode," she said. With that, Starr rose in the air and started flying around the gravel pit. She touched a device on her arm, and a laser beam fired down on one of the old bulldozers sitting at one side of the gravel pit. Almost instantly, it blew into thousands of pieces. Starr then flew up about a thousand feet and went west at hypersonic speed. She immediately vanished from their sight and reappeared from the opposite direction in a matter of seconds. After that, she landed about where she had taken off.

"Starr power…deactivate."

After another flash of light, Starr appeared as she had when they arrived. Matthew looked at the two guests, who were standing there with their mouths wide open. "There's a number of other capabilities of the unit that we have not shown you, such as countermeasures, tracking capability and virtually limitless power. But this should at least give you a feel of what it can do."

"This is incredible," responded the agent. "The possibilities are mind boggling. We'll start thinking about what cases we need assistance with and let you know." With that, they all drove back to Matthew and Starr's house. The two officials couldn't stop talking the whole way.

Before the detective and agent left the Carpenter's home, Matthew had a thought. "Tell you what guys, how about if I rig up a couple of worldwide communication devices that you can use to contact Starr and me in emergencies?"

The official's eyes grew wide. A now very excited detective Taylor responded with, "You really mean it? This will be so…cool. We'll be like those spies on TV shows." He sounded like he was a teenager again. It was quite amusing. In fact, it was so amusing that the entire group burst out laughing.

Matthew and Starr managed to get the communication devices built within a couple of days. It didn't take the officials long to learn how to use them. They had been dealing with technical equipment for many years, so equipment such as radios and GPS locators had become second nature to them.

It was a well-known fact that the first lady, the secretary of state and the attorney general (who were all women) loved shopping together. Other than politics and exotic cooking, it was their favorite pastime. Being out with the girls, having lunch and a few laughs together always helped them to relieve stress. Of course, the fact that the three of them were often together—although convenient for the Secret Service Agents assigned to them—made them all much more susceptible to reporters and generally more vulnerable to outside attacks.

One particularly sunny day, there had been a leak that the three women would be going to a local D.C. area mall. Although the Secret Service knew about the leak, most of them didn't think it would be a problem. One particular agent named Oscar Silverman expressed serious concern to his supervisor, but he was told not to worry about it, as there would be lots of people in the area.

However, as the three women and their agents got out of their cars, a dozen heavily armed men suddenly opened fire from several close vehicles. The Secret

Service agents were caught off guard and most of them were gunned down within seconds. The rest were either killed or rendered harmless within a couple of minutes of exchanging rounds. As might be expected, the women were quite terrified.

One of the terrorists pointed a gun at the women and in a very thick accent said, "You! Get in the car…*now!* Your country will pay dearly to get you back." The women were forced into one of the terrorist's cars, which quickly sped away.

Although Oscar was badly wounded, he was still cognizant enough to pull out his two-way radio and contact headquarters. He pushed the transmit button and, speaking in a broken voice, said, "Emergency! Emergency! This is Agent Silverman. Can anyone read me?"

A crackly voice came over the speaker. "We read you Oscar. Go ahead."

Barely conscious, Oscar mustered all the energy he could. "Ambushed…most agents dead…women kidnapped."

"What's your condition, Oscar?"

"Badly wounded…don't know if I'll make it. Get help." With that, he passed out.

The local police quickly arrived on the scene. Ambulances and paramedics swarmed the area, although it quickly became clear that the only one who had a chance of survival was Oscar. Fortunately, one of the local hospitals had one of Matthew's machines; otherwise, Oscar would probably not have survived.

The police questioned numerous people in the crowd that had gathered after the kidnappers left, but nobody could give a good description of the vehicles or the people. Within an hour, the police set up roadblocks all along the major routes out of the area including D.C., Maryland, Virginia, West Virginia, and Pennsylvania. The kidnappers had wisely chosen to avoid the major highways and use less frequently traveled roads. A few hours later, the terrorists had managed to get to a secluded Virginia hideaway south of Charlottesville.

The blindfolded women were taken out of the car and led about fifty feet away to what appeared to be a house. The terrorists led them through the door and up a flight of stairs, where their blindfolds were removed. The lead kidnapper, whose codename was "Ozone," decided to speak to one of his fellow henchmen.

"Sequoia, remove their blindfolds and take the gags off, but make sure you keep their hands tied."

The other man looked at his boss and replied, "You got it." Even after removing their blindfolds and gags, the women were still uncomfortable, due to having their hands tied.

The attorney general spoke up first. "What about the hands? It's not as if we're going anywhere with all those guns you guys are carrying."

Ozone thought about this for a minute and then spoke to Sequoia. "OK, go ahead and take the ropes off."

Once the ropes were removed, the ladies stretched out their arms and fingers to get circulation back into their arms. Ozone looked at the women and spoke in a very stern voice. "No funny business, you understand? I'd just as soon kill you as keep you alive."

The women reluctantly nodded.

Agent Thompson soon heard about the kidnapping. After working with his fellow agents for about a half an hour, he decided to call Starr. It was about two P.M., and he knew that she would still be in school. He hit the call button on his watch and prayed that all this technology would work and that he would receive a reply.

Starr was in the middle of her final class when her watch flashed. She looked at it for a moment and then spoke into the microphone. "Starr here." Immediately, all the children and the teacher stopped what they were doing and looked at her.

"This is Agent Thompson," came the voice over the watch. "The first lady, secretary of state and attorney general have been kidnapped by terrorists. We have no leads and would request your help in locating and rescuing them."

Starr thought for a second. "I'll need something to help track them," she said. "Tell the White House that I'll be by shortly and that I will need something that the first lady recently touched. A comb or brush with some hair on it would be perfect. I should be there in a few minutes."

"But you're in North Carolina!" replied Agent Thompson in an almost sarcastic voice.

"Yeah, it shouldn't take me very long. Please let them know I'm coming."

"I'll get right on it," the agent responded in a very hesitant but acknowledging voice. "Over and out."

Everyone in the room was still looking at Starr. "Excuse me," she said to her teacher, "but I've really got to run." As she ran toward the door, she turned to the class and said one last thing: "Please pray for the ladies and their families, and please pray that I make the right decisions and bring them home safe."

The teacher and the children were too shocked to know exactly what to do. All they could do was nod in the affirmative. Starr ran out the classroom door, down the stairs and out the exterior doors. As the students watched from the windows, Starr ran down the driveway and said, "Starr power….activate!" The flash was most overwhelming, but when Starr jumped in the air and started accelerating at a high speed, all the students could be heard saying, "Go, Starr, go! Yeah…wahoo!"

Starr accelerated to a speed of more than mach ten and arrived at the White House in about three minutes. The White House security saw her approach and—though they were quite shocked—quite happily met her at the door. Starr was actually quite amazed that the White House Secret Service received the message that fast and reacted as professionally as they did. The agents asked her to wait for a minute while the hairbrush was brought from the President's bedroom. The President himself brought the brush out and gave it to Starr.

"Do you think you can get enough material off this brush to track the kidnappers?" he asked.

"I'll tell you in a minute." Starr held the brush and did an analysis. "I have some very good hair samples here, so I think I'm all set. I'll keep in contact with agent Thompson and let him know the direction and other information as the sensors pick it up. Oh, by the way, please pray for our success."

"That's one you can count on," said the President.

With that, Starr took off. All eyes were on her as she ascended several thousand feet and flew in a big circle in an attempt to get a bearing on the owner of the hair. Her sensors detected a match between the samples and the trail the women took. A few seconds later, there was a confirmed bearing—close to SSW in the direction of Charlottesville.

Starr spoke into her microphone in the suit. "Agent Thompson, I'm getting a direction. It's indicating something below Charlottesville. I should be there within a couple of minutes."

A voice came over the speaker. "Excellent news. I'll start getting some forces moving in that direction and alert the police in Virginia to converge while awaiting more specific directions."

"No need to wait, I'm getting a definite fix. I'll transmit it to you on the watch. At the moment, I've got to rescue the ladies. I'll tell you more after I've got them safe."

Starr flew in the direction of the bearing and accelerated to hypersonic speed. About that time, Agent Thompson responded. "Got the coordinates from you. I'll get them to the police and let the President know that you're on the trail. Good luck, we'll be praying for you!"

By this point, Starr was getting very close to the hideout. With invisibility mode on, she identified six heavily armed guards at different points on the perimeter. One by one, she knocked them out with the unit's heavy stun mode. She then turned her attention to the house. Since she and her father had not yet managed to incorporate the newest mode for walking through walls, she would have to do it the hard way. Sensors indicated that there were nine people in the house; Starr figured that three were the ladies and the rest were the kidnappers.

Fine-tuning the sensors, she saw that the ladies were upstairs in a room with two armed guards while the other four were downstairs. The sensors indicated that the two men in the upstairs room were actually across the room from the women. Starr knew that if she crashed through the window in back of the kidnappers while in invisibility mode, they might be caught off guard long enough for her to take them down. She decided it was time to say a quick prayer.

"OK, Lord, you gave me this ability, now guide me to make the right decisions."

Starr pushed forward and crashed through the window. As the kidnappers turned around, Starr fired on them and they fell to the floor. The poor women didn't know what was happening. Starr could hear footsteps of people coming up the stairs. She thought it would be best to meet them on the stairs instead of having them come into the room and inadvertently hurt the ladies. She quickly ran out of the room and fired on the terrorists as they made their way up the stairs. One by one they fell and tumbled down the stairway.

Starr went back in the room with the ladies and turned the invisibility mode off so that she could be seen. She spoke first in a very calming voice, hoping to assure the ladies and dispel their fears. "It's OK," she said. "I've come to rescue you."

"Who…are you?" asked the first lady. Her voice and manner indicated her complete shock and disbelief.

"I'm Starr Carpenter, code name Starr Gazer. You probably know of my father   he invented the 'healing machine.'" The ladies all thought for a moment, and then the attorney general spoke up.

"Yes, of course I know who he is. I also remember some fancy tale of his daughter being some sort of superwoman." Laughing a little, she finished her remarks by saying, "From what I see, I'm guessing the tale is more fact than fiction."

Suddenly, Starr's sensors showed that an armed person was coming down the hallway. She turned around just in time to see one of the kidnappers turning the bend to come in the door. She fired and stunned him before he could open fire.

"Whew! That was a close one," she said to the three women. "Sorry about that, guess I must have missed one. Let me make sure that the rest of the men in the house are still out cold." With that, Starr went out of the room and saw that the kidnappers were all unconscious. She went back in the room and motioned to the ladies that they should follow her out of the house.

As they were leaving, Starr spoke up. "My sensors are showing that the law enforcement folks should be here within a few minutes. I'll stay with you until they arrive." After they got through the outside door, they could hear the police sirens in the distance. Starr thought it would be best to talk to Agent Thompson at this point.

"Agent Thompson, do you read me?"

"Loud and clear, Starr."

"I have the three ladies under my protection. The twelve kidnappers should be out cold for a while yet. I expect that the police will be here in the next couple of minutes. By the way, you can tell the president that the first lady is doing just fine."

"Excellent news. Talk to you later."

The police cars were now within view. There were six cars, and they screeched in the dirt as they stopped in front of the house. Starr spoke up to the first officer she saw.

"Officer, there are twelve kidnappers in all. There are six in the house and six out here." She pointed out where the various men were. As she pointed out the kidnappers, the officers handcuffed them, woke them up and read them their rights. Additional police cars arrived to escort the three ladies away.

"Thank you so much for saving our lives," the first lady said to Starr. "You truly are a *super girl*." A couple of seconds later she added, "By the way, we'll be in touch."

All three ladies thanked Starr again as they got in the car. As the cars drove off, Starr spoke to the officer in charge.

"Officer, is there anything else you'd like me to do before I leave?"

The officer looked at Starr and replied, "You've done more than enough. I'm sure we can take it from here."

"Fair enough. If you need anything, Agent Thompson knows how to reach me." With that, Starr flew off as the officers and prisoners stood in amazement.

Ozone looked at the officer in charge and asked, "Who is that?"

The officer looked at him with a smirk and replied, "That's Starr Gazer, the most advanced technological wizard of our time and the United States' most secret weapon. You never had a chance, punk."

A few days later, Agent Thompson came to Waynesport Christian School and, along with the principal, walked into Starr's classroom.

"Good day children," said the principal.

All the children were quite attentive and responded with, "Good morning, Mr. Myerhuff."

"Hello, Agent Thompson," Starr added.

The principal looked at Starr and then continued, "This is Agent Thompson with the U.S. Secret Service. He has an announcement for you all."

The principal turned the floor over to Agent Thompson, who walked close to the teacher's desk in order to address the class.

"The president and first lady would like to invite the entire classroom on an overnight trip to the White House. There will be a formal dinner in honor of Starr for saving the first lady, secretary of state and attorney general. You'll need to get permission from your parents before you can go. The President would like you to come this coming Friday night, which is still a few days away. The class does not have to dress formally—the formal part will be for everyone else. The President will have a bus brought here early on Friday morning to take you all to Washington. I'll talk to the principal about the rest of the arrangements."

All the children screamed and shouted with excitement.

Agent Thompson looked at Starr and winked just before he left. Starr smiled, cocked her head to one side and winked back.

When Starr got home from school, she told her family about the trip. Her family already knew, as Agent Thompson had already personally invited them all. That night, Jennifer went out with Starr to look for some formal clothes, as it seemed appropriate that the guest of honor be formally dressed even if the rest of the class was not. Jennifer couldn't believe how beautiful and grownup Starr looked in the new gown. Though she was still only thirteen, she looked a few years older.

When the bus drove up to the White House, the group was met by a horde of people, including the president and first lady, Agent Thompson, and a number of reporters and photographers. Once Jennifer, Matthew and Starr were shown to their rooms, they started dressing for the formal dinner. Jennifer helped Starr get ready. A portion of her long curly blonde hair was tied back in a braid, making her appear much older than she was. Her long formal blue dress was accented with a pearl necklace.

As Starr walked down the long stairs with her parents, she was blinded by the flashes of the photographers. Agent Thompson met the family at the bottom of the stairs and, as promised, ran interference. The family was escorted to the head table, where all the officials were being seated. On one side of Starr sat the first lady and on the other side sat her father.

Starr and her father couldn't believe all the fancy food that was being served. It had to be the nicest dinner that either of them had ever eaten. Starr leaned over and said to the first lady, "This food is incredible. Do you always eat like this?"

The first lady laughed. "No Starr, this is only for our honored guests. Normally we'd just as soon eat yogurt, pancakes, sausage, hamburgers and pizza."

After the meal was over, the dessert was served. There was the most decadent hot fudge cake a la mode that any of them had ever tasted. It was definitely a hit with the children—as well as with most of the adults. When everyone had finished dessert, the President got up from the table and walked over to the podium, which was in front of the head table. All the guests quieted down as the President tapped the podium to address everyone in attendance.

"I'm sure all the children aren't interested in hearing me give a long drawn out speech as I'm normally accustomed to giving, so…in the interest of everyone here, I'll be brief."

Everyone clapped and whistled. The President laughed at their response and then continued.

"I can see already that was a very popular decision. I wish all my speeches would be received as well. As I was saying, Starr and her family have made history by creating a modern day superhero. Saving the lives of some of the most important people in the nation was a feat beyond belief—and all this for someone as young as Starr. To track down terrorists when the rest of the government could not took an incredible mind and a great deal of planning. I personally want to thank Starr and her family for all that they did for the ladies and myself. Heaven knows the government couldn't possibly function without them." Everyone clapped as the President went over to shake the hands of Starr and her family. He then returned to his seat next to the first lady.

The first lady got up next and went to the podium. "I had not met Starr or her family before this horrifying episode. The first look I got of her was when she suddenly appeared out of nowhere after defeating those guards. That was the most harrowing experience of my life, but Starr calmly dealt with the situation as if it were her second nature. The first look I got of her without her suit on was when she got off the bus this afternoon. You would never guess how much of a shock it was to me that a thirteen-year-old girl was responsible for saving my life! I'll never forget this, Starr. Thank you." With that, the first lady left the podium and gave Starr a big hug before sitting down. All the people applauded.

The secretary of state was the next to speak. She got up from her seat next to the President on the opposite side of the first lady, went over to the podium, took a deep breath and began to speak.

"I, too, had never met Starr before. I never even knew that such technology existed. Being someone who is on the receiving end of a terrorist plot and also being someone who deals with diplomacy all the time, getting a firsthand look at what terrorists are capable of gave me a whole new look at how I might handle diplomacy in the future. It also showed me that I should never take life for granted. The tendrils of terrorism affect many people. With high tech communication the way it is, we can see events as they are happening anywhere in the world. This is just fuel to the terrorists, as they know that many people will be watching and their cause will be publicized. The children in this audience will be the future of our nation. It is good that they are here and are getting a view of the government, even if it is only for a day. In closing, I would like to thank Starr and her family for all that they have done for our country and for personally giving me a new outlook on life."

The audience applauded as the secretary of state left the podium. She went to Starr to give her a big hug, and then went back to her seat.

The attorney general was the last to speak. She had a little trouble getting out of her seat, as her dress got caught under one of the chair legs and almost ripped it. Once she freed herself, she managed to get to the podium without further incident. Once the group stopped giggling, she began with a smile.

"Well, at least I didn't need Starr to get me out of that one." The audience laughed.

"It is my job to make sure that people are brought to justice for crimes they commit. But being in the midst of a real plot was something with which I was not prepared to deal. I honestly never thought that the three of us would make it out alive. Even if the U.S. government had given the terrorists what they wanted, it was unlikely that we would have remained alive for long. To be rescued at all was only a dream. To be rescued by a teenager was something I never had imagined. I have a new respect for teenagers and a new love of life. Thank you, Starr, for giving me a new lease on life."

The audience again applauded, although now mostly because all the speeches had been short and to the point. The President then motioned for Starr to say a few words, so she stood up and walked to the podium. "Mr. President and all distinguished guests," she said, "I believe that life is precious and that it should only be taken in cases where you have no choice. My preference is that I stun people, not kill them—the courts can decide guilt or innocence due to the circumstances. I'm sure that there will come a time when I will have no choice but to kill, but I would prefer only to do that as a last resort when I have no other options. Technology is a wonderful thing. It can be used for good or evil. I, like my father and mother, believe in saving lives, and I don't like all the fuss about what we do. I believe that everyone has the ability to provide something to help humanity.

"Each of us grew up in situations that were quite different, and each of us has had unique experiences. We all can share what we know with others. Please think about what you can do to help and then get out there and work to make the world a better place for everyone. Do something to help people you don't even know. Even Jesus said, 'What good does it do us to help our friends? Go help people you know nothing about.' I'm sure you will be hearing more about us in the future, but I certainly hope that everything calms down for now—at least for a few days. I could never perform such feats without the help of the Lord. He deserves all the credit. Thank you for the invitation to come here."

Everyone gave a standing ovation, even the reporters who had seemed skeptical stared in amazement.

Each of the children from the classroom had their picture taken with the president, first lady, secretary of state and attorney general. Starr got some more hugs from each of the ladies and also from the President.

Everyone was tired by the time the evening came to a close, so they all went to bed. Early the next morning, the White House chef prepared a breakfast of crepes, strawberry sauce, and whipped cream. The guests were most impressed, and the children talked about their trip all the way home.

Newspapers around the country ran headlines such as, "Thirteen-Year-Old Girl Saves the U.S. Government" and "Don't Mess with This Teenager." Again, Agent Thompson did a pretty decent job of keeping the reporters away. After the hullabaloo died down, a few months of relative quiet ensued.

Chapter 11

The Invasion

"Hey, Dad," exclaimed Starr as she and her father were finishing up a few more modifications to the suit. "When are we going to try out these cool features?"

Starr and her father had given some thought to a few more technical advances to the suit. These included a way to transport particles without a receiver, a way to rebuild people without Ally, and a way to double the already fantastic speed at which Starr could travel.

"It's already six A.M.," said her father, "and you'll be going to school soon. You'll just have to wait until tonight to start testing." After looking Starr square in the eye, he continued, "Just don't go using them before we finish testing."

"As long as we don't have any major crisis from Agent Thompson before I get back home, I think we'll be OK. Truthfully, I'd be happy if we never had to use them."

"You and me both, my number one daughter. You're fourteen years old, the smartest person there is, and I love you a whole lot."

It wasn't too often that Starr blushed, but this was one of those rare occasions that she turned red. "Aw, dad," she said, "you're getting all mushy on me." With that, she gave him a big hug and they both sat down to watch a little TV before school. The world news was about to start. Matthew and Starr were always interested in keeping up with events because they never knew when they would have to be directly involved.

Matthew had been in the mood for popcorn, so after making a batch he sat down next to Starr just as the news anchor stared to talk. "The country of Harboni has mobilized troops, tanks, planes and other vehicles for what they claim is a massive training exercise," the news reporter was saying. "Many people are skeptical, including the president of the small country of Mern. In an exclusive statement to our local journalist, president Shuli said that he believes Harboni wants to invade them in order to take over their precious gem mines. He believes that they are just using the training exercise as an excuse to mobilize. President Poulini of Harboni was not available for comment, so we'll all just have to wait and see. Mern is a very small country, about half the size of Rhode Island. It has no real army and few defenses. Both countries are on good terms with the United States at the present time."

"What do you think, Dad?"

"Hard to tell. I could see it either way. Like the reporter said, we'll just have to wait and see."

When the news was over, Starr finished breakfast and headed for school.

Starr went to school and the morning passed without incident. She and her friends were having lunch when Starr noticed that Cindy was deep in thought. Starr looked at her with a smile. "Earth to Cindy, Earth to Cindy, are you with us?"

Cindy shook her head and snapped back to reality. "Sure," she said.

Starr looked back and decided that was not a good enough answer. "OK, what's the problem? Do you have some secret admirer?"

Cindy opened her eyes wide. "How did you know?"

"It was just a guess. So who is this prince charming?"

"Well, if you must know, it's Bobby. I think he's fascinated with the fact that I was dead and came back to life. He wants me to go out to a movie with him. What should I say?"

Starr was quite amused but tried to hide it as best she could. "Well, if it were me, I'd try to decide whether I liked him or not. If I didn't like him, the case would be closed."

"Actually, I do like him."

"Then if I were you, I'd ask my parents if it were OK for the two of you to go out."

"Do you really think I should?"

"Only you can answer that one. If I were you, I'd pray about it."

"I thought you'd say that."

Starr's first class in the afternoon was world history. The class had barely started when her emergency phone rang. She and her classmates all looked at it as she hit the answer button.

"This is Starr. Go ahead."

"Starr, this is Agent Thompson. The country of Harboni has invaded the tiny country of Mern, and the president of Mern has called our president for emergency help. There is already major devastation and chaos. Our president has requested your assistance."

Starr looked a bit puzzled. "What do you want me to do?"

"The President said that it would take most of the day to even get a few of our planes and troops in the area. He is requesting that you do what you can to slow down the enemy until help arrives."

"You want me to stop an entire army and air force by myself?"

"The President is just asking that you do what you can. The country of Mern is being overrun and lots of lives are being lost. If you can help, that will be a few lives saved."

"Who kicked off the invasion?"

"Most likely Yuctar Poulini, the current dictator of Harboni. He's a pretty ruthless guy."

"OK, I'll survey the situation and see what I can do. I'll be in touch once I see how things are going. Over and out."

Starr looked at her classmates. "Wish me luck, guys. Maybe I'll get lucky and come back with some diamonds for the class." When they didn't respond, Starr decided on a different approach. "I believe that the best thing you could do is pray for me, the people of Mern, and the people of Harboni."

"We will Starr," said the teacher.

Starr got up from her chair and went to the front of the room. "Starr power…activate!" she said. Within seconds she was suited up and ready to go. "Set coordinates for the capital of Mern. No specific location. Shields on. Invisibility mode on. Energize."

Immediately, Starr disappeared from the room. This left the occupants staring in amazement, as they had never seen Starr leave via transport mode before.

Starr materialized in downtown Mern during an explosion of a mortar round. She was unhurt by the explosion, but it startled her for a second.

"Yikes, that was close. I need some altitude to see what the deal is." Starr hit a device on her arm and shot up about 2,000 feet. What she saw was truly overwhelming: There were hundreds of airplanes firing missiles, shooting people in the streets and blowing up buildings. Tanks were coming in from everywhere and destroying anything and everything in their path. It seemed as though president Yuctar Poulini intended on leveling the entire country and taking no prisoners.

Starr took a deep breath and said, "Well, I can't let them take any more lives, so here it goes. Set weapons for destruct." She fired on the first airplane and it blew up into what appeared to be thousands of pieces. The remnants of the ship came down in a ball of flame.

"That wasn't so bad. Let's see if I can work on more than one at a time."

She fired on five planes simultaneously, blowing each of them up with pinpoint accuracy. Within half an hour, she had eliminated every Harboni fighter and bomber that was in the air within one hundred miles. Her sensors did not indicate that there were any more airborne aircraft in either Harboni or Mern.

One of the Harboni generals came into the war room and started talking to president Poulini. "Mr. President," he said, "our planes are being blown out of the sky. We have no idea who is doing it or how. There is nothing on the radar that we can see."

"What about the ground forces?"

"They have not yet been touched."

"Find out who or what is doing this, or I will have your head."

"Yes, Mr. President."

The general left the room, leaving President Poulini alone with his thoughts. He started thinking to himself about which country would have the technology to wipe out his entire air force in such a short time. He knew better than to call any foreign governments, as that would only place him in a very awkward position. As it was, if he just could complete the invasion and destroy the entire country, there would be nobody left in Mern to accuse him.

Once Starr finished destroying the planes, she started working on the tanks, armored vehicles and ground troops. "So far, this is much easier than I thought it would be. I should recharge before I continue."

With that, she said, "Starr power…recharge." Within seconds, an influx of power placed her at maximum power. Within another hour, all the Harboni tanks had been destroyed and the troops had been obliterated. Starr surveyed the destruction and realized that the poor Mernites wouldn't have had a chance. As it was, if she had arrived there a few hours earlier, it would have made a huge difference.

Then, out of corner of her eye, Starr saw a sight that made her want to cry. A woman who was obviously a Mernite mother was crying over what appeared to be her teenage son. The young man lay bleeding in the street. This touched Starr so much that she decided to go see what she could do. She landed near the mother and became visible again. The mother looked up and spoke in her native Mern language. Luckily, Starr had her built in two-way translator on.

"Are you going to kill me too?" the woman was saying. "Isn't it enough that you have killed my son?"

Starr knew that the poor woman was out of her senses with grief. She felt true Christian love for the woman and responded, "It was not I who killed your son; it was the Harboni government. I was sent here by the United States government to help stop the bloodshed. Now let me look at your son to see what I can do."

The poor woman was in tears. "Didn't you hear me? He is dead!"

"There is a possibility that I can do something. Let me try."

Starr went over to the boy, bent down and placed her hands on him.

"Computer, analyze the boy and access the damage. Stop any more deterioration."

After what seemed like ages—but was actually only about twenty seconds—the computer responded.

"Analysis complete. Patient has been dead about five minutes. Although patient has been stabilized, his brain function has deteriorated about 53 percent."

"Provide whatever power is necessary to rebuild patient. Recharge if necessary."

"Acknowledged."

A glow came from Starr's hands and the boy's body started to change. Places where there were holes from shrapnel were now being repaired. Within a few more minutes, his physical body looked normal.

"Brain function has returned to normal," the computer said. "Memory has been brought up to 97.8 percent."

"Good. If that's the best we can do, we'll have to live with it. Return heartbeat and respiration to normal."

"Acknowledged."

A few seconds later, the computer provided an additional response. "Rebuilding complete."

Starr removed her hands and the boy opened his eyes. He looked at his mother, and they reached out to each other and started crying. Starr got up and looked around. There were bodies strewn all over the street. She realized that there was only so much she could do for them at this point. The mother looked up at Starr. "I don't know who you are, but I thank you from the bottom of my heart. If there is anything I can do for you, tell me."

"As a matter of fact, there is. Could you please direct me to president Shuli's mansion?"

The mother pointed. "It is about five kilometers in that direction."

Starr thanked her and took off into the air. She soon arrived at what was left of the mansion. She had been by there a little earlier while taking out tanks and Harboni soldiers but hadn't paid much attention to where the mansion was at the time.

There were people milling about in total despair. Many of them looked to Starr like the zombies she had seen in TV movies. She landed and asked one particular gentleman if the President happened to be all right. The man indicated that as far as he knew the President had survived, and as he looked around he pointed to a man a couple of hundred meters away. The President had seen Starr land and had started walking over to her with some of his cabinet and a few armed guards.

"Mr. President, I'm Starr Carpenter from the United States," Starr said when the President approached.

President Shuli nodded. "Yes, I have heard stories of you from the news reports of the United States."

"I believe that I have taken out all the Harboni aircraft, tanks and soldiers that were threatening you. Is there anything else I can do here before I go after President Poulini?"

Just then, Starr's sensors picked up a lone fighter coming in from the north.

"Excuse me, Mr. President. Looks like I missed one."

Within a few seconds, all the people on the ground could see the fighter in the distance. As people started to run for cover, Starr fired on the approaching plane, which was still about two kilometers away, and blew it to pieces. The President, his cabinet and his personal bodyguards were astonished at what they saw.

Starr turned to the President. "As I was saying, is there anything else I can do here?" she said.

The President looked at Starr with an expression of extreme sadness. "You have done amazing things here. We are indebted to both you and your country. If only you could have saved my wife."

Starr perked up. Realizing the importance of the timing, she quickly responded, "Where is she?"

The President pointed. "She is lying over there about one hundred meters away."

"Let me see if there is anything I can do."

The President led Starr over to his wife, who was lying in the street.

"She has been dead for more than half an hour."

Starr leaned over the woman, who looked about forty years old, and placed her hands on her. She then spoke to her computer. "Computer, analyze the patient and access the damage. Stop any more deterioration."

"Acknowledged."

The computer analyzed the woman and responded within about thirty seconds.

"The patient is not dead. Pulse and respiration are at minimal levels. A lung has been punctured by shrapnel and several internal organs have been torn."

"Can you repair the damage?"

"Affirmative."

"Begin repair."

"Acknowledged."

A glow came from Starr's hands, and within a couple of minutes the woman started to breathe easier. Within a few more minutes, her body looked normal. Except for the blood on her clothes, it would not have been possible to think that she was anything other than asleep. The woman opened her eyes, saw her husband and smiled.

Starr breathed a sigh of relief and then looked at President Shuli. "I believe your wife should be fine."

The President and his wife embraced. With tears in his eyes, the President replied, "I am at your disposal.

What you did for me was more than I can repay. What can I do for you?"

"Actually, you could give me the probable location of President Poulini."

The President wiped the tears from his eyes and composed himself. "I'd say he is in his bunker about twenty kilometers southwest of the capital. It is disguised as a resort hotel. He would be in the lowest level underground."

"Well, that helps, thank you. With any luck, I'll see you within an hour." With that, Starr took off and headed for the Harboni capital at hypersonic speed. President Shuli's wife looked at her husband and asked, "Who was that?"

"She is Starr Carpenter from the United States. I never really believed all the stories I read about her amazing feats. We are indebted to her and her country—not only for saving our country, but for saving all of our lives." The President looked at his wife and gave her a loving smile. "Most of all, she brought you back to me."

The President kissed her like he had not seen her in years.

Starr had not traveled far before she realized that enabling the invisibility mode would be a smart idea. Then she started thinking about what to do next. "Hmmm. What do I do when I meet him? Should I capture him or kill him? If I leave it up to the U.S. government, they'll bring him to trial and it will take forever. I think the best choice is to bring him to President Shuli in Mern. The crimes that President Poulini committed were against that country, so they should decide his punishment."

Starr flew for only a few minutes when she arrived at the area President Shuli had described. "Sensors on maximum," she said. "Now let's see if we can find that hiding spot that President Shuli described. If I remember right, I should be looking for a deep underground area."

After about fifteen seconds she said, "That looks about right—there, about 300 meters down. Let's see if I can make it a little easier on myself and start breaking through the ground and come in from the side at an angle instead of from the top." With that, she started firing continuously at the ground at an angle. The ground easily broke apart and she made a rather decent tunnel.

From inside the bunker, President Poulini, his advisors and security staff were suddenly quite concerned. They could hear tremendous explosions and what appeared to be drilling. The reports that had come back to the President and his staff indicated that all the Harboni fighters and bombers had been destroyed and that all their tanks and armored vehicles had also been destroyed. Fear came over them all. The sound rose to the point of being deafening and then suddenly stopped.

Starr decided to recharge one more time before entering the bunker. Once recharged, she decided to see how close she really was. The wall was within a meter of her current location, so she decided that it was time to finish blasting through the wall. Sensors indicated that there were eleven people inside, most of whom were heavily armed.

"OK, no time like the present to push forward. I'm not going to be able to take them all prisoner, so I'll have to kill most of them if they fire on me. Regardless of what happens, I'm taking Poulini prisoner."

With that, she fired, blowing a big hole in the wall where President Poulini and the others were located. Although everyone was caught by surprise, they still opened fire on Starr with their handguns. As expected, the bullets had no effect. Starr opened fire on the cabinet members and the security force and then looked around for President Poulini. The description that President Shuli had provided fit one man to a tee. When Starr had eliminated all the people except the President, she spoke.

"President Poulini, I presume. I have destroyed all your planes, tanks and all the military forces that you assembled against Mern. President Shuli asked the United States for help, and I was asked to stop your invasion. I am taking you prisoner back to Mern to stand trial for invasion and murder."

President Poulini pulled out his gun to kill himself, but Starr quickly stunned him, dropping him to the ground. "Sorry Pres," she said, "you're coming back alive."

Starr picked up the President and dragged him back out of the hole and up to the surface. After getting there, she put President Poulini on her back and headed toward Mern. Although it was a little awkward and she couldn't quite travel as fast as she had when she came, she still made it back within half an hour. Starr thought it best to go back to where she had left President Shuli, since it wasn't likely he'd have gone very far with all the people wanting his attention. Starr saw him standing next to his wife, surrounded by all his bodyguards. His look was one of sheer disbelief as he saw that Starr had President Poulini in tow.

After Starr landed, President Shuli spoke. "If I had not seen it with my own eyes, I would not have believed it."

"Here is your adversary, President Shuli. He's all yours. His generals and staff have been eliminated and won't bother you anymore. Is there anything else that I can do before I go back home?"

"You have done more than enough. It is up to us now. We will begin the rebuilding process. My guards will take hold of this attacker." The guards laid hold of the just-waking President Poulini and dragged him off to prison.

"I'm sure that the United States will provide support within the next few days. I expect that you can hold out until then."

"Yes, we should be fine. Thank you once again for all that you have done."

"I, too, thank you for giving me back my life and my husband," said Mrs. Shuli.

Starr waved goodbye and walked off a little distance before calling Agent Thompson.

"Agent Thompson, this is Starr."

"Go ahead, Starr. We've all been wondering what has been going on."

"All the Harboni tanks, fighters, bombers and troops have been destroyed. I have taken President Poulini prisoner and have handed him over to President Shuli. At this point, I'm ready to come home. Truthfully, I'm kind of tired. What these countries really need at this point is a cleanup crew in Harboni and a rebuilding crew in Mern."

It was obvious from the silence over the communicator that Agent Thompson was in shock. After about fifteen seconds he responded with, "You really are incredible."

"Just doing my job, sir. I'm about to transport back. I could use a little R and R."

"Sounds like you really deserve some time off. Come on home."

Starr told the onboard computer to transport her back home. In a flash, she was gone.

Chapter 12

Framed

Starr came home from school one day all excited. "Dad, what do I do? I think Jeff likes me!"

"OK, sit down and tell me all about it."

"Well, since I came back from Mern a few months ago, Jeff's been eyeing me pretty good. I don't think it's that he just likes blondes, either. He's from a Marine family, and he started the school year here after coming from Camp Pendleton in California with his family. He heard about my capture of President Poulini, and I think he's got a crush on me."

Matthew thought about this for a few seconds and then smiled. "You'll probably want to have a good talk with your mother, but at least for the moment, you should just be the normal friendly girl that you've always been. Chances are, he'll hang around you more and more as time goes on."

A couple of weeks later, Jeff decided to get up enough courage to ask Starr to go to a movie and out for pizza. After asking her mom and dad, Starr accepted the invitation. Ironically, although Starr could perform amazing feats as Starr Gazer, she was not allowed to drive a car. Though the U.S. government could have easily vouched for her, Matthew and Jennifer wanted Starr to grow up like any other girl her age and do regular teenager stuff at the appropriate time.

Jeff and his mother picked up Starr, and they drove to the local theater where Jeff's mother dropped them both off. Since the pizza joint was almost next door to the theater, Jeff arranged to call his mother on the family cell phone when they were done eating. When the movie was over and they were waiting for their pizza, the two teenagers began to talk a bit more freely. Jeff decided to break the ice and start the conversation.

"I can't imagine what it's like to not need any sleep. What do you do with all your time?"

"Well, because my dad doesn't need sleep either, we do a lot of talking and a whole lot of inventing."

"So what was it like to capture President Poulini? Did he put up much of a fight?"

"Actually, he and his generals shot at me at point blank range, but it didn't do much good because I had the force field on. After I eliminated his entire security force, President Poulini didn't quite know what to do. He figured that his only real choice was to commit suicide to avoid prosecution. Luckily, I managed to stun him before he finished himself off."

Jeff's look was partially one of being overwhelmed and partially one of admiration and love. Once he came back to his senses, he responded, "That's incredible. I really admire you." This made Starr blush—not necessarily because of what was said, but because of who was saying it.

Being from a Marine family, Jeff was taught to be honorable. Seeing Starr blush, he immediately responded with, "I'm sorry, I didn't mean to embarrass you."

Starr was most impressed that Jeff was so sensitive. She composed herself and then responded, "That's OK. I'm just not used to discussing my work adventures with someone my own age. Most don't have a clue what I'm talking about."

That made Jeff laugh, and once Jeff began laughing, Starr started laughing as well. A few seconds later, they were both roaring with laughter. Once they had both calmed down and wiped the tears from their eyes, Jeff thought it best to break the ice again.

"So, do you have any plans for future enhancements or adventures?"

"Actually, I'm letting the Lord decide that for me. He'll tell me what He wants me to do at the appropriate time."

Jeff had accepted Christ and understood the answer that Starr had given. In fact, Jeff was so impressed with the answer that he knew that he had found the right girl for him. It would be just a matter of time before he would ask for her hand in marriage—although that would still be a few years away. Jeff thought it would be good to let her know that he too let Christ lead his life, so he decided to direct the conversation in that direction.

"It's nice to hear you say that. Ever since I accepted Christ and began reading the Scriptures, I listen to the Lord when I pray and let the Lord direct my life."

Starr could have been pushed over with a feather. She'd never heard anything so wise from a person her own age. As she was about to respond, she suddenly received a call from Agent Thompson that snapped her back into reality.

"Starr, this is Agent Thompson."

"Go ahead."

"Detective Taylor's wife was killed and he's being blamed for the murder. He was in court today and the evidence is really pointing against him. The jury is out deliberating at the moment. I don't think they'll be back until morning."

Starr was shocked and took a few seconds to reply. "Oh, no! Susie was such a sweet person. I don't think Michael would ever do such a thing. What do you want me to do?"

"Truthfully, I'm not sure. I was hoping that you could think of something that might help."

"I'll talk to Dad when I get home. Maybe between the two of us, we might be able to come up with a plan."

"Thank you. I'll talk to you tomorrow. Over and out."

"Goodbye, Agent Thompson."

Starr looked up at Jeff with concern on her face. "I'm really not sure what to do."

Jeff thought for a moment and then looked at her and said, "The only real way to know what happened would have been to be there when Susie was murdered. Then you would know exactly what happened."

Starr looked up bright eyed and said, "Jeff, you're a genius! You deserve a kiss for that."

Now it was Jeff's turn to be speechless, but he managed to respond, "Thanks, but I don't think I said anything amazing."

"Oh, but you did. It's absolutely perfect. I'll go back in time in invisibility mode—not to change history, but just to take a digital film of what actually happened. Then I can show it to the judge and jury and we'll at least know the truth of what happened."

Jeff was excited but a little puzzled. "You can do that?"

"Sure! One of the first things that Dad and I incorporated into the Starr Gazer unit was the time warp mode." Starr then paused for a moment and a look of concern passed over her face. "But what if Detective Taylor really did it?"

Knowing that Starr needed some advice, Jeff responded in a loving manner. "I know that the Lord would want you to find out the truth. I'm sure He will provide the strength you need when you need it."

Starr smiled and reached out to hold Jeff's hand. "Thanks, I needed that."

The two teenagers were soon interrupted by a waitress who wanted to place the pizza on the table. Starr and Jeff continued to talk while they hungrily ate their pizza and drank their soft drinks. Occasionally they stole glances at each other in a very awkward but loving way.

When they were finished, Jeff paid the bill and called his mother to come pick them up. When Jeff dropped Starr off at home, she turned around and gave him a kiss on the cheek and said, "This is for the movie." She gave him a kiss on the other cheek and said, "This is for supper." She gave him a small kiss on the lips and said, "This is for the idea of going back in time."

Jeff just stood there with a glazed look on his face. As expected, he was now the one who could have been knocked over with a feather. After he recovered he said goodnight, and then Starr ran into the house to talk to her father.

Matthew was watching the news and looked up when Starr walked in.

"So, how was the big date?" he asked with a smile.

"I'll tell you about that later," Starr replied with a concerned look on her face. "Right now I've got something really important to tell you."

Matthew could see that Starr was troubled, so he turned his full attention to her.

"OK, honey, calm down and tell me what's going on."

When Starr finally calmed down, she began to relate the story. "Dad, Agent Thompson called and said that Detective Taylor's wife has been killed. They're blaming Michael."

"Oh, no. Do you have some idea of where to begin?"

"Jeff thought that if we could have been there when it happened, we would know who had committed the crime. I stared thinking that I could do a time warp, figure out who really did it and then record the event. After that, I can go to court and show the jury what really happened."

"Sounds like a good idea."

"Jeff really gets the credit for this one. He's a real neat guy and loves the Lord. I'll tell you about that later. Right now, I've got to work fast—the jury is currently deliberating, and although it's nighttime, they could come out at any minute. I need to be prepared."

Father and daughter hugged each other, and then the elder Carpenter responded. "If I were you, I would get going."

A moment later, Starr recited the activation words. In an instant she transformed, disappeared and almost instantly reappeared. All she could say to her father was, "Wow! You wouldn't believe it."

Just then, a voice from her communicator spoke. "Starr, the jury just came back," said Agent Thompson. They pronounced a guilty verdict. You need to get here right away if you have anything important to add to the case."

"Understood, Agent Thompson."

Matthew gave her the thumbs up. After a flash, Starr was gone. A split second later, she appeared in the courtroom. Some of the people screamed when she appeared, and the judge called to the bailiff to maintain order. Starr looked at the judge and spoke.

"Pardon me, your honor. I'm Starr Gazer." Immediately the courtroom became quiet as people stared and listened. "I recently learned of this case and decided to investigate on my own. If you are willing to give me a few minutes, I can present some evidence that will change the verdict."

Once the judge regained his composure, he responded to the request. "This is highly irregular, but since you are such a highly distinguished visitor—and in the spirit of finding out the truth—I will allow you to present your evidence."

With a confident look, Starr bowed to the judge. "Thank you, your honor. I've developed a method to time warp without altering history. What I did in this case was travel back in time, observe and record the actual events as they happened, and then travel forward in time to the present in order to show the events to the court. Would showing the events as they actually happened be acceptable evidence to the court?"

The judge looked at the prosecution and the defense. "I believe that if we have the chance to hear evidence that could change the outcome of the trial, we should hear it while we are all still here. Does either the prosecution or the defense wish to say anything to Starr Gazer before she begins?"

"No, your honor," said the defense attorney. The prosecuting attorney thought for a split second and then replied, "I would like to know the details of how this time travel was accomplished."

Starr looked at the prosecuting attorney. "Nobody asked for the details when I stopped the war between

Harboni and Mern single-handedly and saved the lives of millions of people. Nor did anyone ask for details when I saved the first lady, the secretary of state and the attorney general from the kidnappers. Based on the government security clearance I have, you frankly have no true *need to know,* as leaking that information could jeopardize national security. And since the prosecution is actually part of the government, I don't believe you would be acting in the best interest of the country if I were to give you that information."

The prosecuting attorney looked at Starr and nodded. "OK, Starr, you win. Let's do our job and find out who really killed Mrs. Taylor."

"All right, Starr," said the judge. "Let's see what you have for evidence."

In a grateful but confident manner, Starr responded, "Thank you your honor." She looked at the crowd and began. "Ladies and gentlemen, what you are about to see is real. It may be too graphic for some people. If you feel that you might have a problem with this, you may want to leave the room. I would also ask that the police secure the room, as the real killer is actually here. I would also like to address the real killer at this time: You will not escape, as I can easily catch you. Any hostages that you would take and harm I could easily heal. In short, you can either give up now or wait until I am finished. In either case, you're through."

Nobody moved a muscle. All eyes were fixated on Starr.

Starr continued, "Although we might like to change history, that in itself would likely cause a paradox. In the end, all we can do is see what happened and learn from it. OK, your honor, I'm ready to start."

The judge nodded and Starr moved closer to the blank wall to the left of the judge and raised her hand. "Behold the events of the past. The time on the lower right will be the actual time the events happened."

With that, a cloud formed on the wall; as it cleared, the Taylor home was in view. The judge, jury, prosecution, defense and the rest of the people in the courtroom were fully engrossed in the events that were taking place. As they all watched, a car pulled into the driveway and Detective Taylor got out. He walked into the door of the house and was met by Susie and Detective Callahan.

"Hello, dear," said Susie. "Paul stopped by, and I invited him to dinner."

Detective Taylor shook the hand of Detective Callahan. "Hey, buddy. What's up? How's that new case you're working on?"

In a rather downcast yet sarcastic voice, Paul replied, "Actually, it's coming along very slowly. I don't work as quickly as you do…especially when you get help from the Feds and that wonder girl."

"Oh, you mean Starr Gazer?" Michael replied. "Yeah, she helps out a bunch. I couldn't do nearly as well without her help."

"Don't I know it," Paul murmured under his breath.

"Did you say something, Paul?"

"Nothing important," responded Paul in a very innocent tone.

Michael poured himself a glass of water for dinner, placed it on the table and then excused himself
while he stepped into the kitchen for a minute to help
Susie. Paul looked to see if the coast was clear and then
took some tablets out of his pocket and put them into
Michael's glass. The tablets fizzed for a moment and
then disappeared.

After a few minutes, Michael came out of the kitchen,
took a few sips of water from his glass and began walking
back toward the kitchen. As he approached the door, he
collapsed to the floor. Paul immediately went over to
Michael. Taking a clean handkerchief from his pocket,
he pulled Michael's gun from out of its holster.

Paul called out to Susie in a very concerned voice.
"Michael collapsed on the floor! Come here quickly!"

When Susie came through the doorway, Paul shot
her with Michael's gun. She collapsed to the floor and
a pool of blood began to form. After several minutes,
Paul went over to her and checked her pulse to make
sure she was dead. He then walked over to Michael and
placed the gun in his hand to make sure that Michael's
fingerprints were all over it.

Paul got up to leave. "Now I'll be the big cheese in
the department," he said. "You won't be solving crimes
any more...buddy." With that, he left the house.

Back in court, Starr closed the window to the past.
"The pill that Detective Callahan gave to Detective

Taylor not only knocked him out but also erased his short-term memory," she said to the court. "That is why he had no recollection of what had happened that day and was unable to defend himself." Everyone looked at Paul Callahan, who was now crying.

The judge called to the bailiff. "Take charge of Mr. Callahan. Based on this new evidence, does the defense or the prosecution have anything to say?"

Both attorneys simultaneously answered, "No, your honor."

The judge looked at the jury. "Does the jury wish to deliberate any more?"

"No, your honor," said the foreperson for the jury. "Based on this evidence, we the jury find the defendant *not guilty*."

The judge looked at the court and with one pound of the gavel declared, "Case dismissed!"

Detective Taylor looked at Starr and managed a small wink and a smile. Starr realized that he was really hurting from the loss of his wife, Susie. She transformed from Starr Gazer back to her normal appearance, which startled the courtroom. Starr walked over to Michael and gave him a hug.

"Thank you, Starr," said Michael. "You saved my life and my sanity. I didn't know whether I killed Susie or not. Without your help, I might have gone on for the rest of my life thinking I might have killed her."

Starr smiled at him. "I didn't know what I would find in the past, but I knew that I had to find out the truth for all of us." With that, Starr said goodbye and transported herself home. As she arrived, all of her family was sitting in the living room.

"So, how did everything go in court?" Matthew asked.

Starr looked at her family and responded, "You might want to sit down for this."

After Starr finished the tale, Matthew held hands with Jennifer and spoke to Starr and Andrew. "Children," he said, "we have something to tell you. In about six months you should have a little brother or sister. Your mother and I are quite happy about it."

Starr and Andrew were ecstatic. They jumped up and down and gave hugs to each other and to their parents. Andrew smiled and looked at his parents in a very stern yet childlike way. "It better be a girl, because I don't feel like sharing my room."

The whole family just looked at each other. First Starr began laughing, then Jennifer, and finally Matthew. Eventually, Starr looked at Andrew and said, "I don't know about you, but I'll take whatever the Lord gives us. It's not as though Mom and Dad are going to give it back."

Andrew thought about this for a few seconds and then replied, "I guess so. Maybe having a little brother that I can teach the ropes to will be pretty cool after all."

Tears of laughter could be seen on everyone's face for quite a while.

Chapter 13

The Slave Trade

Starr couldn't believe how time flew. She was almost seventeen. Her little brother, whom she totally adored, was already two years old, and she spoiled him rotten. When she wasn't at school or working on cases, she was babysitting him.

One Friday while at school, Starr's friend Pauline approached and said, "My parents are going off for the weekend and I'll be home alone. I'm going to have a sleepover tonight and was hoping you could come."

Starr sighed. "Oh, rats! This would have to be the one weekend that my parents and Andrew would be gone. They're leaving as soon as I get home."

Pauline was disappointed, but she soon perked up when she had another idea. "Any chance you can get someone else to watch the baby?"

Starr knew where this was going. Being a very responsible teenager, she responded, "I wish, but my parents would have my head if I didn't watch him. Sorry!"

The two friends left school and went in opposite directions. Pauline went to prepare for the sleepover while Starr went home to babysit for the weekend.

That night, Pauline had ten of her friends from school over for the weekend. At around 10 o'clock, the girls had not yet changed for bed—in fact, they were still watching horror movies and screaming at everything that happened. The neighbors had been warned that Pauline was having a slumber party and should expect a little more noise than normal.

The Jasmines were a local gang that did almost anything for money—money they usually used to buy guns, knives and drugs. They had recently been approached by a gentleman who went by the code name of "Skylark" who talked to them about making big money in the white slave trade. All they had to do, he said, was capture some unsuspecting girls, bring them to a predefined rendezvous point and help load them into a truck. The rest was up to Skylark.

Spike, who was the head gang member, had learned about the goodie-two-shoes girls who were having a sleep over. He decided that this would be a great opportunity to make a lot of money fast. So on Friday night, Spike took five of his gang members and went over to Pauline's house. They went to the back of the house, where they heard lots of screaming. Spike checked the back door and found that it was open.

Pauline had not yet locked all the doors, so she couldn't have made it any easier for Spike and his gang. And since the girls had planned to spend the entire weekend together, nobody would be looking for them until at least Sunday afternoon. For Spike and the Jasmines, it was the perfect setup. With a smile on his face, Spike said, "What a break. They're making this easier than we thought! We're going to sneak in. Make sure that they don't escape from any of the other doors, and above all else, don't damage the merchandise—regardless of how tempting it may be. We will get paid more if everything is intact. Got it?"

Although there was some grumbling at first, all the gang members eventually shook their heads in agreement. Spike looked at the rest of the gang. "Let's go."

Six members of the gang opened the back door of the house and crept into the kitchen. They could see the girls through the doorway. They were all in the living room and were facing the opposite direction from the kitchen. The boys took out some chloroform and doused a few cloths with it. They waited for a point in the movie where the girls screamed and then slowly crept into the room. One member went behind each girl and quietly placed the cloth over her mouth and nose, rendering her unconscious.

The gang caught the girls totally by surprise. Although they could only chloroform a few girls at a time, the others were in such shock that they just sat there and screamed. Within a couple of minutes, all the girls were unconscious.

"I know this is tempting, guys," Spike reminded his gang, "but we made a deal with Skylark. Don't touch the merchandise."

The boys carried the girls outside and placed them in their van, propping them up so there would be enough room for all of them. They shut off the lights in the house and locked all the doors, just in case anybody came snooping. By the time they drove off, it was close to ten forty-five P.M.

One gang member named Josh spoke up. "Hey Spike, I think this is the best caper we've ever pulled off. We left no trace of anything. No fingerprints, nothing. I don't even think Starr Gazer could track us this time."

"I don't think she would get involved in anything like this. She only gets involved in international affairs."

"Yeah, but I think some of the girls we kidnapped may have been friends with her."

"We'll worry about that later. She's just another girl."

"Yeah, but she doesn't sleep."

About an hour later, the van took a turn onto an old deserted road and drove out to an abandoned airstrip. As the group came to a clearing, there was an airplane waiting for them. It was a small jet capable of carrying about fifteen people. The gang loaded the girls (who were still drugged, tied and gagged) onto the airplane.

A gentleman who was standing nearby handed Spike an envelope with some money in it. Spike counted it and nodded his head as though he were quite pleased with himself. The gentleman watched all the girls being loaded on the plane and then said, "You have done very well this time. The merchandise looks very, very good. Let us know when you get some more."

Spike winked and shook his head. "Sure thing, boss."

By the time the plane was in the air, the girls had started to stir. There were two Asian men in the cabin beside the pilot and copilot. The girls tried to scream, but it did no good. Many of them started to cry.

One of the Asian men was in his late thirties. With a smirk on his face, he said to the girls, "Do not worry my little ones. If you obey your new masters, you will be treated very well. You will make fine breeding stock."

The girls couldn't believe what they were hearing. They didn't know whether to scream or cry. In the end, they did both.

It was mid-morning on Saturday before the plane arrived in Brazil. The plan was to unload the girls and place them on a larger plane bound for the Orient. The plane landed on schedule and parked close to other planes of similar size. As the girls were carried out, they could see other young girls of different nationalities being brought onto the much larger plane. This plane was an older commercial plane and could carry about 180 people. Once the girls were brought on board, it became obvious to them that the ones who were already on board were just as frightened as they were. The plane had six seats across, but the middle seats of the plane were not being used in order to allow for some amount of comfort for the girls who were still bound and gagged.

Once the bigger plane got in the air, the gags were removed and girls were untied. It was going to be a long flight, so it was necessary for the girls to eat and move around. The girls were watched by several men with guns, who gave them sandwiches, apples and cans of soda.

Pauline began talking to some of the girls from the other countries. It was a good thing that she paid attention in Spanish class, as the majority of the girls were from Spanish-speaking countries and few could speak English. Their stories were similar to hers. They had been kidnapped before they knew what was happening to them and loaded onto the plane bound for the Orient.

An hour before landing—which was not until almost four P.M. Sunday local time (four A.M. Sunday EST)—the girls were again gagged and their hands were tied. Struggling was not going to do much good, as a gun was pointed at each of their heads. Once they landed, the girls were ushered into a big dormitory and allowed to sleep until about six A.M. the following morning (six P.M. EST Sunday).

Back in the United States, no one knew about the kidnapping until Sunday afternoon, when the parents realized that they had not heard from their children. When four o'clock came around, the parents began calling Pauline's house. When they received no response, the parents began to drive to the host house for a look. By five P.M., ten of the girls' parents were standing on the front lawn of Pauline's house. About that time, Pauline's parents came home.

"Hey, what's all the commotion about?" asked Mr. Snyder.

One man who was about the same age as Mr. Snyder said, "We came to pick up our daughter, but there doesn't seem to be anyone here."

"Well, we'll just see who's home," replied Mr. Snyder.

Mr. Snyder pulled some keys out of his pocket and opened the front door. All the parents walked into the house one by one.

"Pauline, where are you?" cried Mr. Snyder in a very loud voice. All was quiet in the house. There was no response.

"OK, everyone," said Mr. Snyder. "Spread out and search the place."

The parents searched upstairs, downstairs and outside the house. There were no notes and everything looked in pretty good shape. The Jasmine gang had cleaned up so as to leave no trace of their crime. Even the TV had been turned off.

"I don't like the look of this," said Mr. Snyder. "I think we should call the police."

The police arrived about ten minutes later. When they didn't find anything, they called Detective Taylor out to investigate. Detective Taylor questioned the neighbors and found out that the girls had a pretty wild party on Friday night.

"Yes, officer," said one neighbor. "There was quite a lot of commotion Friday night. Lots of yelling, screaming and general ruckus. Pauline had come by earlier and indicated there might be some noise but that they wouldn't be up past midnight."

"So…what time did the yelling stop?"

"I'd say about 11 o'clock."

"What did you see yesterday?"

"That's the funny thing. I didn't see or hear anything at all from that house."

"Nothing?"

"Absolutely nothing."

"What about today?"

"Didn't hear anything today, either, until all these people started showing up about an hour ago."

"Thank you for your time." A puzzled Detective Taylor walked slowly back to the Snyder's house.

On the other side of the world, Pauline and the girls were just waking up. After they shook the cobwebs off, they were ushered to breakfast in a very large room.

"What's going to happen to us?" asked Pauline's friend Sue.

"I don't really know," said Pauline. "We're somewhere in Asia, and I think we're going to be sold somehow."

"You mean…into slavery?" asked Sue.

"I'm afraid so. Oh, where's Starr when I need her?"

After breakfast, an Asian woman in her mid-forties addressed the crowd of girls through an interpreter that had been provided for each of the languages the girls spoke. "I'm sure you are all scared and wondering what will happen to you. You are probably safer here than you would have been at home. Here you will have few worries. You will have someone who will care for your needs. All you will have to do is please them. Now, line up over here and you will be given a set of clothes that you will change into. It is not like you have any choice. The guards will make sure that you comply. Notice that the guards are women. They have guns and are not afraid to use them. You can place your old clothes in a pile on the floor."

Although the girls didn't want to comply, they didn't really know what other choice they had. So, reluctantly, they changed clothes. Surprisingly, the new clothes were extremely comfortable—in fact, they were the most comfortable clothes the girls had ever worn. The clothes were very modest and were similar to floor-length dresses with high neck tops. After changing, the girls were assembled into a group. The woman who had previously addressed them spoke again.

"You all look very beautiful. In a short time you will be going to your new homes. Obey your masters and it will go well with you. If you do not, you will be severely punished. You are all very pretty, and we would not like to see your beautiful faces disfigured."

If the girls were not scared before, they were definitely scared now.

Back in the United States, Detective Taylor was coming to the conclusion that this was not an ordinary kidnapping, as there had been no request for a ransom. As he looked at his communicator watch, he slapped his forehead with his hand, realizing that it was high time to call Starr.

Starr's family had just come home from their trip and were in the midst of unloading the car. Starr went out to meet them. "Glad to see you all back," she said. "It was pretty quiet. There were no calls, and nothing exciting happened."

"Well, that's a first," said her father, quite surprised. He hadn't finished getting out his last word when Starr received a call from Detective Taylor on her communicator.

"Go ahead, Detective Taylor."

"Your friends were having a sleepover and they've disappeared without a trace. The neighbors indicate that there hasn't been any noise at the Snyder's house since Friday night at around eleven P.M. There is nothing out of the ordinary here—no sign of a struggle, no forced entry, no fingerprints of anyone on record."

Although Starr was quite shocked, she knew that she should be levelheaded and deal with the task at hand.

"I'm on it. I'll let you know when I find something. Over and out."

Starr looked at her father. "Looks like I spoke too soon. I think I'll take a quick look at the past and find out what happened. Then I'll start tracking them down."

Starr quickly transformed into Starr Gazer and time warped to the past Friday night at Pauline's house. Once she had witnessed the events firsthand and knew that it was the Jasmine gang who had taken the girls, she returned to the present. Starr thought that it was time to call Detective Taylor.

"Go ahead, Starr."

"I warped back in time and discovered that the Jasmine gang took the girls. I didn't stay to figure out where they went. Do you have any clue as to the Jasmine's whereabouts?"

"Spike, the leader of the gang, works at the local body shop. He would probably be at his home right now or out with the gang. We'll put out an APB on all of them."

"Good. I'll start looking for him as well. I'll stay in touch."

"Me too. Over and out."

It didn't take Starr long to find the boys. It was well known that one of their hangouts was close to the local movie theater. Starr appeared in front of Spike and his gang in a flash of light that caught them completely by surprise. Starr looked directly at Spike.

"OK, Spike, what did you do with the girls?"

"Well, if it isn't goodie-two-shoes," said Spike. "Girls? What girls?"

"Don't play with me, bozo. I warped back in time and saw the whole thing. I just didn't stay long enough to see where you took them."

Spike looked at the other boys. "Time to have some fun, guys." The whole gang pulled out their guns and knives and started to go after Starr. Starr opened fire on all the gang members except Spike and knocked them out in a split second. She then looked back at Spike. "This can be easy or hard. It's up to you."

Spike tried to grab Starr, but all he got was a heavy shock from her force field. Starr just shook her head. "OK, buster, here goes."

There was a quick flash of light and Spike fell to the ground. This light stun was intended to allow Starr to question him. She grabbed him by the shirt and pulled him toward her.

"All right, now. Where did you take the girls?"

Although Spike was barely conscious, he was now quite willing to talk.

"Brought them to a waiting plane. They were taken to the Orient. Skylark knows all the details."

"Who's Skylark?"

"He's a professional in the slave trade."

"How do I find him?"

"His number is in my wallet."

Starr looked through Spike's wallet and found the number. She stunned Spike again to knock him into a long-term sleep and then called Detective Taylor. "Spike and the boys are out cold in the alley next to the theater," she said. "He's working for a slave trader named Skylark. Got anything on him?"

"We've heard of him, but we've never been able to track him down."

Starr gave Michael the phone number. "I think I have a plan," she said. "Tell you what, you call Skylark using the watch phone and I'll trace the call and pay him a visit. What do you think?"

"I'm game."

"OK, let me know when you're ready."

Michael called Skylark and Starr traced the call. As soon as Skylark answered, Starr appeared before him in a flash. There were several people in the room, and all were taken aback by her dramatic entrance. Starr noticed how each was dressed and soon picked out who was in charge. She spoke with unprecedented force and urgency.

"Skylark, I presume? You've got exactly five seconds to tell me where the girls are that the Jasmine gang gave to you."

The men ignored the demand and opened fire on Starr. As one would expect, the bullets had no effect against her high-tech force field.

"When will they ever learn?" said Starr, shaking her head. In an instant she had stunned all of the men except Skylark. It was obvious from the look on his face that he knew he was cornered. Starr moved toward Skylark and with her right arm pointing toward him said, "If you want to remain alive, you'll tell me where they are."

"Very well," Skylark replied in a sarcastic voice, "though it will do you no good. By now they are likely in hundreds of homes, pleasing their new masters. But if you must know, the plane went from here to Brazil and then to Beijing. I don't know the exact location."

Starr seemed pleased with the response and decided that she'd spent enough time there. "That'll have to do for a start. Now to put you to sleep for a while." Skylark fell to the floor with a thud after he had been stunned.

Starr next called Michael with the information and told him where to pick up Skylark and his cohorts. In an instant she transported herself to Pauline's house to look for something that would help her track down Pauline once she arrived in Beijing. When she appeared in Pauline's house, everyone screamed.

Starr quickly located Mr. Snyder. "Mr. Snyder, I need something of Pauline's that I can trace her with. It could be hair…anything that was part of her."

Mr. Snyder thought for a moment and then his face lit up. "I think I've got just the thing. It's some of her baby teeth."

Mr. Snyder ran off and found several of Pauline's baby teeth, which they had kept in a little jar. Mr. Snyder gave them to Starr. "I hope these work for you. Do you have any idea where the girls are?"

"I believe they are in China. I'll have to hurry. The more time I waste is that much more time they could be in trouble." With that, she thanked Mr. Snyder and disappeared.

Starr reappeared in Beijing at around 1,000 meters above ground level. Within seconds, she activated the locater to find Pauline. The signal was quite strong and indicated that Pauline was about twenty-three kilometers to the southwest.

Starr made it to the coordinates in a matter of seconds and saw a large building. Turning on the invisibility mode, she quickly appeared inside. Once there, she was overwhelmed by the sheer number of girls that she found. She spoke to herself as she tried to come up with a plan to rescue the girls.

"Let's see, there are probably a couple hundred girls here. There are tons of heavily armed guards…hmm… I'd say about twenty. Looks like the girls have started walking toward one of the doors." After surveying the situation, she thought to herself, "Oh, I see, there are buses outside. Most likely they're ready to take the girls to their slave quarters. It definitely looks like I got here just in time. If I can get Pauline to calm the other girls down, I think I can get the guards out of the way."

Once she found Pauline, she whispered, "Pauline, it's Starr."

Pauline whirled around. Not seeing anyone there, she whispered, "Starr, where are you?"

"I have the invisibility mode on. I'm going to start taking these guards out, but I'll need for you to calm the other girls down. When I say "*now*," tell the girls to lie on the floor, because I'm going to start firing."

As quick as she could, Pauline passed the information to the other girls and then came back to where she left Starr. "OK, I'm ready," she whispered.

As Starr yelled out, "*Now!*" Pauline yelled in a loud voice, "Everyone! Hit the floor!"

The girls quickly fell to the floor, which caught all the others in attendance by surprise. Before the guards could react, Starr opened fire and took out ten of them before they knew what happened. The remaining guards and the woman leader didn't know what to do. Because Starr was still invisible, she made short work of the other ten. Starr then turned her attention to the leader, who was quite paranoid by now as she was the only one left in the room with all the girls. Starr appeared and addressed the leader.

"You have been a very bad girl. I'm taking these girls out of here and back to their homes whether you like it or not. Are you going to cooperate, or am I going to have to kill you where you stand?"

The woman became indignant. "Who are you? You cannot get far. I have a whole army to help me."

"Do you remember the war between Harboni and Mern? I single-handedly stopped that entire war. I could annihilate your whole army in a matter of minutes."

Although the woman seemed a little uneasy, she quickly regained her composure and said, "Oh, so you are the famous Starr Gazer."

"That's me…in the flesh. I honestly don't care who you are. So…are you going to cooperate or do I take you out where you stand?"

The woman laughed and said in a highly sarcastic tone, "You and these girls will never get back to your country alive."

"You don't know me very well," Starr replied. She paused and then continued, "Suit yourself, loser. I'm taking these girls home whether you like it or not.

You're not going to destroy their lives or mine. Enjoy your time in hell."

With that, Starr finished her off. She then looked at all the girls and decided it was time to call her father.

"Dad, I've found all the girls. It looks like there are a couple hundred here. How do I get them all back?"

Matthew thought for a second and replied, "I'll widen the transport beam so that you can send about ten at a time. Let me know when you're ready."

"OK, Dad. I'll just need to call Detective Taylor so that he can start making arrangements to pick up all the girls. I'll also let you know when I've got enough girls to start transporting."

Starr next called Michael. "I've got a couple hundred girls all wanting to go home. I'm going to send them to my house. Can you start making arrangements to get them categorized and sent back to their own homes and countries?"

"I'll get right on it, Starr."

All the girls were formed into groups of ten. There were twenty groups in all. Starr called her father and indicated that she was ready. Once her father had responded that he was ready, Starr pointed her right arm at the first group and said, "Commence transport."

Within a couple of seconds the first group of girls disappeared. Pauline was placed in the last group so that she could help organize the girls. The first eighteen groups transported without a hitch. However, as Starr was about to transport the nineteenth group, several armed men suddenly appeared at the door and raised their rifles up to fire. Starr looked at them and said,

"Sorry guys, not today." After she fired on them, they fell to the floor.

Firing on the walls above the doorways created a large amount of rubble, effectively sealing off the doors. This bought Starr a little more time. Looking at the rest of the girls, she said, "OK, let's continue where we left off."

As soon as the nineteenth group departed, a huge blast suddenly ripped through the wall, sending rubble within a few feet of them. "Pauline, go hide the girls in the far room over there!" Starr cried as soon as the dust had cleared. She pointed to a room about fifty feet away. "I'll be there as soon as I can."

Pauline led the other nine girls to the far side of the big hall where there was a small room and shut the door. A tank slowly began pushing its way into the building along with about a dozen armed soldiers. Starr went into invisibility mode and took the tank out first. The tank blew up with such force that all but two of the soldiers were killed. Taking care of these two only took a few seconds for Starr. Although soldiers could be heard outside, Starr thought it best to get the rest of the girls safely home before taking on the rest of the Chinese military.

Just as Starr finished transporting the rest of the girls, a blast knocked part of the wall down where she was standing. If Starr had not had the force field on, she would have been killed. She left the building while still in invisibility mode. As she looked back, she saw hundreds of troops approaching the building that she had just left.

"Looks like this may be a good time to call Agent Thompson," Starr said to herself.

"Agent Thompson, I've broken up a Chinese white slavery ring, but it appears that it is backed by the government. Please call the President and have him immediately call the communist party leader and recommend that he call off his army before I personally deliver them to him in pieces. They kidnapped about 200 girls. I've transported them back to the U.S., but it doesn't appear that this army likes losing. Detective Taylor has some more details if you need them."

"I understand, Starr. I'll get right on it."

Looking at the tanks, armored vehicles and soldiers, Starr decided to take out as many as she could until she heard back from Agent Thompson.

Detective Taylor was having problems of his own. Even with the help he had received, he was still having trouble keeping track of all the girls. He called in reinforcements from a few counties, including several social service agencies. Part of the problem was what to do with the girls that were not from the United States. He contacted the Immigration and Customs Enforcement and requested assistance but was told the soonest help could arrive was the next day. In the meantime, Detective Taylor managed to get some rooms at a nearby hotel for all the children whose parents could not pick them up that day.

When the last of the girls arrived, Pauline was among them. She and her parents saw each other at about the same time.

"Pauline!" her father said.

"Mom, Dad, it's so good to be back."

"Where's Starr?"

"I'm not sure. The last thing I knew she was trying to get us safely home before taking on the entire Chinese army."

After Starr had eliminated all of the enemy in the area, she received a call from Agent Thompson.

"Starr, the communist party leader regrets any misunderstanding his government may have had. The ringleader had misled the party and had all the military at her disposal. The party leader is currently recalling all of his soldiers and will be directing them to seek out any lingering slave traders. He has assured our President that any remaining slave traders will be sought out and that any slaves found will be returned to their countries of origin."

"I get the impression he's trying to save what's left of his army. I'll hang around for a few more minutes and see if I can find any other girls that were not part of this wave before I come home. Tell Detective Taylor I'm OK and that I'll be back in a little while."

"I understand. We'll see you when you get back. Uh…as usual, good work."

Starr felt like she needed to pray about any possible girls that may need her help. "Lord, I feel that there is someone still out here that You still want me to help. Please direct me to her. In Your Word, You say that if I give You credit, You'll direct my paths. Right now I could use some direction."

When Starr looked around, she saw a strange light coming from a house across town. Deep down she had a feeling that she needed to check this out. After arriving, it turned out that the light was a reflection from a car mirror. Starr was getting a strong sense that this was the right area to search and decided that a thorough investigation would be in order. Her sensors indicated that the house across the street contained a girl who appeared close to the floor. Using her onboard systems, she electronically opened the door and walked toward the room where the girl was. Because the door was locked from the outside, Starr felt that this was the most likely place that her captors had put her. After disintegrating the lock, the door easily opened.

What Starr saw inside almost made her cry. There was the girl, about 14 years old, chained to the bed. Her shoulder-length hair hadn't been washed in weeks and she appeared to be malnourished. The girl was scantily dressed and had bruises on her face, arms and legs. Although Starr couldn't be sure, it appeared as if the girl had been on her knees, praying. As the girl looked up and saw Starr, it was obvious that she was frightened.

"Don't be afraid, I'm not going to hurt you," Starr said before the girl could get a word out. Once the girl realized that she would not be beaten, she calmed down enough for Starr to continue.

"Were you kidnapped in the United States? Are you now being held here as a slave?"

The girl seemed quite surprised that the stranger knew about her circumstances.

"Yes, how did you know?"

"I'm Starr Gazer. You and I were praying at about the same time and the Lord led me to you."

As the girl started to cry, Starr put her arm around her shoulders and helped her up. It only took a few seconds for Starr to remove the chain from the girl's leg. She looked the girl in the face, gave her a big hug, and smiled before speaking again.

"What's your name?"

"It's Jennifer."

"That's my mother's name. Well, Jennifer, I think it's time to get you back home."

The two girls heard the front door open and a sound like someone entering the house. Starr knew that it was likely the girl's master. Jennifer heard the sound and cringed.

Seeing the effect this had on Jennifer, Starr said, "Don't worry. I'll take care of this."

When the man saw Starr, he grabbed a nearby sword and ran at her with a very mean look on his face. However, Starr stunned him with a single blast and sent him flying across the room. The man landed on the couch, quite unconscious.

With that taken care of, Starr again turned her attention to Jennifer.

"Jennifer, can you tell if you're badly injured?"

"I don't think I've been hurt too badly, although these bruises really hurt. One thing strange is that I've been feeling really nauseous lately."

On a hunch, Starr decided to do a quick medical analysis. Her hunch was correct: the poor girl was pregnant. Other than that and a few nasty bruises, she was basically all right.

"He abused you pretty bad, didn't he?" said Starr.

Jennifer shook her head in the affirmative.

"How long have you been acting as a concubine for that guy?"

"Ever since I got here, about five months ago."

"Did you realize you were pregnant?"

"I started thinking that I might be."

Starr gave her another hug. "It's OK. The Lord heard your cry and sent me to rescue you. Like I said before, let's get you home."

Starr spoke into her communicator. "Detective Taylor, are you there?"

"Right here, Starr."

"The Lord led me to another girl who has been here for some time. She's pregnant and could use her family, some medical care and some friends."

"We'll take good care of her, Starr. We'll await transport."

"Thanks, Michael."

Starr looked at Jennifer and told her that she'd meet her back in the United States in a little while. With that, Starr sent Jennifer on the short trip around the world.

Before heading for home, Starr decided to get a little altitude and see if there was anything else that she needed to do. Feeling that everything had now been taken care of, she transported herself back home.

In a flash, Starr appeared back at her own house. There were people everywhere: police, people from the rescue squad, people from ICE (who happened to get there earlier than expected), a couple hundred girls, some of the girls' parents and lots of reporters. Starr quickly transformed into her normal self and went to talk to Pauline.

"Pauline, how's it going since you all got back?"

"Pretty good. I think we all survived the ordeal. We at least got some real comfortable dresses out of the deal."

The two girls hugged each other and laughed.

"Do you know where that girl is that I transported last?"

"I think she's over there talking to your mother."

Starr went over and gave her mother a hug. She then turned and smiled at Jennifer.

"I'll bet you don't recognize me without my getup on."

"Actually, I recognized you by your voice."

"How are you feeling?"

"Like I'm really free. I know that I have a lot to think about with the baby. I'm already thinking about adoption. I have my whole life ahead of me, and I'd like to get back to normal as soon as I can."

"I think you'll do just fine."

Starr felt someone come up behind her and place two hands over her eyes. "Guess who?" the voice whispered.

"Jeff!"

She wheeled around and gave him a big hug. "Weren't we supposed to have a date tonight?"

"I think you're right. You up for Chinese food?"

They looked at each other and burst out laughing.

Chapter 14

The Plot

At five years of age, Starr's baby brother, Luke, had his older sister wrapped around his finger. She adored him, and he thought she was just the best.

One weekend, Starr remained home while the rest of the family went to see Matthew's parents. They left on Friday and were to be gone for more than a week. Starr was now twenty years old and starting to wonder if Jeff would ever propose. They had a date Friday night, and she hoped that it would finally be the time. Jeff knocked on the door to pick her up, and she quickly ran to the door.

"Hello, beautiful," said Jeff. "You ready yet?"

"Just sticking on my shoes now."

"That old movie should be pretty funny: *The Creature that Took Over the World.* What do I have to worry about with the most powerful person in the world sitting next to me?"

"You're just buttering me up. But…I do accept the compliment."

They both laughed as Starr finished putting on her shoes. Jeff held out his hand to help her up from the chair and stole a kiss as they met.

"That's no kiss. Now *this* is a kiss." She proceeded to give him the longest one she ever had.

Jeff was dazed for a moment and just replied with a big, "Wow."

Their date had not been as eventful as she had hoped, and he dropped her back home about ten thirty P.M. She went into the house and though she didn't need any sleep, she decided to go to her room, say her nightly prayers and do some reading.

Once there, she saw the flowers Jeff had brought her and decided to play a game with the daisies. "Let's see, he loves me…he loves me not…"

Members of the anti-religion group No More Religion (NMR) were talking one day at a meeting in Maryland. One of the members named Kevin got up and addressed the assembly. "Religion has caused most of the world's problems since the beginning of time," he said. "If we could get rid of all religious activities in the world, it would be a much better place. Religious people are very superstitious. I recommend that we talk to similar organizations in other countries and come up with a common plan of action to get rid of them that we can carry out simultaneously."

"You mean, like a revolution?" said a young man named Harold.

"That's right. We'll start by eliminating all the churches, and then we'll work on the people. We'll even blot them out from history so that there won't be any record that religion ever existed."

"Now you're talking, dude."

The whole group clapped with excitement. One older man in his sixties got up and said, "I've been wanting to do something like this for a long time but I've never had the chance. But I do have one question: What do we do about Starr Gazer?"

"I've thought about that, too," said Kevin. "She's not always protected. All we have to do is figure out when she's most vulnerable and then blast her to smithereens."

Applause was heard all around the building.

Kevin divided up the tasks, including who would talk to people in which countries, who would arrange for the explosives, and who would organize the various factions in the United States. Planning for the entire set of activities took about two years, and by the time everything was organized, subgroups had been founded all over the world. Finally, the day came when the plans were to be carried out. It was set for 11 P.M. EST on Friday.

When the day had finally arrived, Kevin addressed the large crowd of followers. "Today we are performing the world a service like none other. We will finally have peace in the world, because there won't be any religious factions to get in the way and fight against each other. We will get rid of them all."

The crowd cheered for a whole minute before Kevin hushed them.

"Let us go to our respective posts and do what we came to do."

Kevin and a small group of people went out of the room, got into an SUV and drove the couple of hours to where Starr lived. It was now ten forty-five P.M. and Kevin knew they didn't have much time to get ready. Each of the men had hand grenades, automatic weapons and a few small rocket launchers. They surrounded the house and waited for 11:00 P.M. to arrive.

Luke was a very clever boy for his age, and his parents knew it. His grandmother had just given him his very own Study Bible in large print for him to read when he grew older. He had just started to read and was already learning about Jesus and the various parables.

"Now, Luke, what do you think of your new Bible?" his grandmother asked.

"I think it's just great, grandma. As soon as I can read more, I'm going to be a Sunday school teacher."

"It's nice of you to think that way. It'll take you a few more years before you can teach."

"OK, grandma. I'll learn until my brain can't hold any more."

His grandmother laughed. "Whatever you do, just don't lose your new Bible."

It was a few seconds before 11 P.M. Kevin raised his machine gun, aimed it at Starr's bedroom window and said, "Goodbye, Starr Gazer!" With that, he opened fire, and the other men who came along with him did so as well. Hand grenades were thrown into her house, and soon the entire place was set ablaze. In the background, the sounds of additional blasts coming from churches being destroyed could also be heard.

Starr never knew what hit her. The first shots hit both her head and her chest. The hand grenades took off her right arm and one of her legs. Her body collapsed to the floor. It was several minutes before her heart totally stopped. Ally was blown apart, as was the computer equipment that the family had in the house. The house was going up in flames, and there was nobody around to help.

All around the world, there was total havoc. Churches and religious people were being killed. It didn't make any difference what religion it was—all were treated the same. There was so much destruction and chaos occurring that the police didn't know where to start to control it. By the time the president and leaders of the world countries called out their armies, a lot of damage had already been done.

Luke heard the noise and saw how upset his family was about all the churches being destroyed. So he grabbed his Bible, a small metal box and a small shovel and ran outside to bury the Bible so that nobody could find it but him. He ran out into the field with a flashlight, dug a hole in the ground, and then buried the box with the Bible in it.

"Nobody's going to get my Bible," said Luke.

When he was done, he came back into the house and stayed with his family.

The medical staff at the local hospital where Starr's family lived had not yet received any casualties and didn't really know what was going on. They had just shut down Abby for the night and left the room. The communicator that Starr had was still intact. The communicator and the implant acted as monitoring devices for Starr so that if anything happened to her she would be immediately transported to Ally. Luckily, Starr's father had the foresight to arrange for Abby to be the backup in case anything happened to Ally. If Ally did not respond within a minute, Abby would immediately activate, even if powered down.

Once Abby sensed that Starr was no longer alive, the unit came back online. A voice from Abby spoke just as if there were people in the room with whom she needed to communicate.

"Emergency. Emergency. Transporting Starr Gazer."

Within a minute, Abby continued. "Analyzing."

After what seemed like an eternity—though it was only another minute—the voice over the speaker said, "Analysis complete. Patient has severe brain damage, a severed right arm and severe internal damage. Current internal power is insufficient for repair. Contacting additional units Mary, Noreen, Paula, Rachel and Stephanie for assistance."

After about twenty minutes, Abby began to speak again. "Repair complete. Reassembly beginning."

About thirty seconds later, Starr appeared on the table within Abby. She opened her eyes and got up.

"Abby," she said. "You are a sight for sore eyes. Looks like you did a pretty good job of putting me back together."

"Units Mary, Noreen, Paula, Rachel and Stephanie were required for assistance due to the power requirements."

Starr laughed and replied, "You still did a great job. Please relay that to the other units."

"Understood."

Starr got up off the table and after a few big breaths said to herself, "Well, time to figure out what's going on and put a stop to it."

With that, Starr transformed into Starr Gazer and left the hospital. Fortunately, Jeff had recommended to Matthew and Starr that they not keep all the Starr Gazer equipment at their home, so they had asked Agent Thompson to make a special building repository underground to house it in.

"I'll have to thank Jeff when this is all over for saving our equipment."

Starr contacted Agent Thompson and found out what was going on. The governments of various nations had begun to respond, but much damage had already been done. Starr couldn't be everywhere at the same time, so she let Agent Thompson set the priorities.

The NMR groups, like terrorists, were hard to track down because the members did not appear to have a real base of operations. Over a period of months, between the efforts of law enforcement and Starr, approximately 75 percent of the members of the NMR groups were captured or killed. Numerous NMR members went into hiding once the crackdown began. Kevin, who never was captured, contacted some of the leaders of the other factions and told them to lay low. He instructed them to teach others in the way of the rebellion so that one day they could begin again—and this time succeed.

One particular crackdown that Starr was involved with revolved around a small nonresistance church in western Maryland. Starr had been in the area and had seen some suspicious smoke rising on the horizon. She quickly arrived on the scene, where she saw some characters escaping in an SUV.

"This looks promising," she said to herself. "I'm sure that if they're legit, they won't mind my stopping them."

When Starr landed in the middle of the road, the driver went directly for her. With a few quick shots, she disabled the vehicle. When the group tried to escape on foot, she lightly stunned them so that she could question them.

"What's the deal?" she said to the driver. "Why are you so intent on killing innocent people?"

Although the driver was groggy, he still managed an answer. "You religious people have been fighting for years. Once we eliminate all of you, there will be peace."

Starr looked at him and replied, "You cannot have complete peace without God. People would wander around without any real purpose in life. There would be total chaos until marshal law was instituted. Then people would be forced to live in a militarized state where everyone was monitored, and anyone who did not comply with the government would be eliminated. Is that the kind of life you want?"

"You're crazy. As soon as all you hypocrites are gone, there will be peace."

At that point, the police showed up and took the prisoners away. Starr decided to go check out the area around the burning building to see if anyone needed help. When she arrived, she saw that several people had been severely wounded and two people had been killed. The rescue squad was there and confirmed the death of the two before proceeding to help the others. Starr immediately went to the two people who had died.

"Let's see if I can do anything for you two."

When she had completed a quick analysis, she decided that she would try to save their lives. Starr beamed one person to Abby and the other to Mary. She would have worked on them herself, but she knew that she needed to see if she could determine the extent of the injuries of the others.

Starr went to one older woman who looked to be in her sixties and said, "Let me have a look at your wounds. I think I can probably help you out."

The woman looked at Starr and responded, "We are a peace-loving people. Why would anyone want to hurt us?"

"People are a strange lot," Starr said as she began to work on the woman's wounds. "They will fight for a cause but not realize they may be causing a worse problem than the one they are trying to solve. People have done it in the name of religion, and now they are doing it to try to get rid of religion."

It took about a year for the Carpenter's house to be rebuilt. Once it had been completed, many of the family's friends were invited over for a party. At the party, Jeff mustered up enough courage to speak.

"I've been thinking about something for quite a while and have just now got enough courage to do it." Jeff took Starr by the hand and said, "I don't know whether you'll have me, but I'd like to spend the rest of my life with you. So...will you marry me?"

Starr looked at Jeff with her hands on her hips and her head cocked to one side and replied, "I've been waiting a long time for this. What took you so long?"

Jeff, a little surprised and a bit unsure of her response, answered her with, "Uh...should I take that as a yes?"

"What do you think?" Starr replied with a smile.

Everybody laughed and clapped.

Luke ran up to Starr and jumped into her arms. "Does that mean I could be an uncle someday?"

Starr and Jeff looked at each other, smiled, and then looked back at Luke. All Starr could say was, "Could be, munchkin. Could be!"

Part 3

Return to the Light

Chapter 15

The Discovery

Mark was a scientist. Not just any scientist, you understand—he had doctoral degrees in everything from biology to nuclear physics. People would come from miles around just to ask his advice on the most advanced topics. He had given more seminars than he could remember. But today was a special day. It was July 23, 2543, and today was his 55th birthday. His wife, Catherine, was about to surprise him with a party when the doorbell rang.

"Mark," said Catherine. "Could you please answer the door?"

"All right, dear," replied Mark.

As soon as Mark opened the door, he was shocked to see some of his friends and coworkers that he had not seen in years. Standing there were John, Katie, Mitchell, Hubert, Alfred, Jack, Betty, Paul, Ivan, Sandy, Tom and Vicky. Mark was completely overwhelmed.

"Surprise!" said John. "Happy Birthday."

They all rushed in and sang Happy Birthday to him, at which point Catherine came over to Mark and gave him a big kiss. Mark was so shocked that he didn't know what to say.

John was the first one to give Mark a present.

"Where in the world did you find a slide rule, old chum?" asked Mark. "I haven't seen one of these in years!"

"I happened to be visiting an old shop in Brussels and came across it. I knew you'd like it for your collection."

"You were certainly right about that." After inspecting the slide rule for a minute, Mark said, "It is a fine specimen." With that he shook John's hand and said, "Thank you so much, my friend."

"You're entirely welcome."

Katie brought in the cake and jokingly said, "I don't know if I can get fifty-five candles on this thing. I may have to put two groups of five on and leave it at that."

With a big smile Mark replied, "I'm embarrassed enough as it is. You don't have to make it any worse by placing fifty-five candles on it! I'm sure that two groups of five will be fine."

Mitchell brought in a 700-year-old German mantle clock. Mark was very impressed. "I never thought I would have one of these for my own," he said. "This is quite a surprise. You know, if I ever get that place in the country I've always wanted, I'll be sure to place this clock on the fireplace mantle."

Before Mark knew what was happening, Hubert was bringing in an 800-year-old English roll top desk made of real wood.

Mark laughed as he declared, "I don't know when I'll ever get there, but I won't have to buy a thing for that country house!"

He hadn't even finished his sentence when Alfred brought in an old Tiffany lamp. Then Jack brought in an old Persian rug, Betty a cast iron cookware set, Paul a seventeenth-century French love seat, Ivan an eighteenth-century American hutch, Sandy an eighteenth-century cuckoo clock, and Tom a nineteenth-century Austrian bed frame. Vicky made several trips to bring in food, including a strudel, homemade rolls and a Hungarian Goulash. Finally, Catherine brought in a big box wrapped in birthday paper with a very big bow. Mark opened the note that was attached to the package. It read:

To my loving husband,
May you always find what you truly seek.
Your loving wife, Catherine

You could almost see a tear in one of Mark's eyes. "I don't know what this is," he said, "but with a note like this, it could even be a can of beans and I'd be thrilled to death."

The entire group laughed as Mark carefully removed the bow and the paper and opened the box. To his surprise, inside was another box. When he opened that box, there was another. Inside that box was one more. Finally, when he opened the last box, he found an envelope.

"With all this work I've had to go through, this has to be good." Taking a deep breath, he opened the envelope and found a piece of paper with a survey plat. "Why, it's a deed with my name on it. It doesn't look like just any deed, either—it's a deed to a one hundred-acre place in the country. Well, I'm quite shocked."

Mark was about to go looking for something when Catherine handed him a folded piece of paper. "Is this what you're looking for?"

Mark looked at the paper, smiled, and replied, "Yes, dear."

Catherine knew that he would want to know the exact location of the property, so she had handed him a map with the exact spot circled. Mark looked at Catherine with a smile on his face and then gave her a kiss. He was as speechless as he had ever been in his life.

The party continued for some time. By the time it was over, Mark and Catherine were both bushed.

"Although I'm pretty excited about the property, I'm in no shape to be traipsing off on a good hike without some sleep."

"That is an excellent suggestion, my husband," a very tired Catherine replied. "I don't expect that the property will move very far before tomorrow."

"You always could make me laugh, honey."

With a little smile she responded, "I know."

After breakfast, Mark and Catherine set off for the country in their All Purpose Vehicle (APV). This particular APV could drive on land, fly in the air and move on or under water. It had an excellent Vertical Take-Off and Landing (VTOL) system, which they used to shorten the trip. Because the vehicle could travel at a speed of more than mach one in the air, the 653-mile trip did not take them very long. When they got within range, Mark could see from the air the survey flags that had been placed around the property. Only then did he realize exactly how big the area was. There was a five-acre pond, some open fields and a nice woods with a stream running toward the back of it. Mark landed the APV, and he and Catherine got out and began walking around.

"This is the place I've always wanted," Mark said.

After a few minutes of walking around, Mark decided to ask his wife a few questions. "Catherine, where do you think would be the best place to put a house?"

"I had actually given that some thought. I think that the best spot would be right over there close to that clump of trees."

"Nice choice. That does seem like a nice spot for a house. Any thoughts on a garden?"

"How about over there about fifty meters to the right of the house. There's a lot of light there and the soil looks in decent condition for a garden."

"I've always wanted some animals and a pond of fish. Any preference on types?"

After a minute or so, Catherine replied, "I think catfish, pickerel, large mouth bass, and maybe perch would do best in this fresh-water environment. I don't think trout would do very well here, however. Also, a few cattle and a dairy cow or milk goat would be nice.

A few llamas or alpacas might be cute, and a couple of goats to keep the brush down might also be helpful."

"We've been married for thirty years," said Mark, "and I never knew that you were such an expert on animals. I guess I'll just have to wait and see what other surprises you have in store."

They both laughed and then prepared to head back home.

As the months passed, the house and the barn went up, the property was fenced, and the pond was stocked with fish. All the furniture that Mark and Catherine's friends had given to them was placed in their new country home. By the time they were finished the home was impeccable, cozy and quaint.

One day in the spring of 2544, Mark decided that it was high time to plant a garden. He bought some seeds for peas, carrots, radishes, cucumbers, tomatoes, peppers, eggplant, squash, pumpkins, watermelons and lettuce. Catherine was intent on planting an herb garden of her own. She bought bay, chocolate mint, lemon balm, thyme, parsley, sage, and rosemary plants. Together, Mark and Catherine bought some fruit trees, including apple, pear, apricot, plum, cherry and peach.

Once the fruit trees and herb garden were planted, Mark thought that it would be best to next work on the vegetable garden. He had never planted anything quite so large before, so he wasn't quite sure how to begin.

Catherine was about fifty meters away, so he had to yell out, "Catherine! Do you have any ideas on how to begin this garden?"

About that time, Mark heard the sound of a farm tractor.

"Yes dear!' yelled Catherine in reply. "I've hired a man who's coming on that tractor to help."

Mark smiled and said, "I knew there was some reason I married you!"

Catherine blew him a kiss and then continued to work in the herb garden. Within a few hours, the garden had been plowed and the rows had been laid. Mark then went about the task of sowing the seeds, covering them and marking the rows so that he would know where he planted each vegetable.

As Mark was hammering in the last marker, he hit something quite hard. Thinking it was just a rock, he moved the marker over a little and tried hammering in again. Whatever it was, it was still there. It sounded as if metal were hitting metal instead of rock.

"Well, this seems a little odd. It's got my curiosity up now, so I might as well try to figure out what it is."

Mark dug and dug. He found the edge of the strange metal object and then dug down around the sides. With a great deal of strain and sweat, he finally loosened the object and pulled it out of the ground. It was a metal box that was quite rusted but otherwise intact.

"Hmm…this looks interesting. From the looks of it, I'd say it's been here for several hundred years at least." Mark tried to open it, but found that he could not. "Just my luck the thing would have to be locked.

I don't have anything to pry it open here, so I may as well bring it back to the house where I have decent tools to do the job right."

Once inside the house, Mark was able to break the lock by using a hammer and a crowbar. As he attempted to open the box, he soon realized that the hinges were rusted and were not going to cooperate. However, after considerable effort, he succeeded in breaking them open.

"Good! Now I should be able to just lift the top off and see what treasure I've found."

What he found astonished him—it was just a book. He dusted off the cover and noticed that the book had the words "Holy Bible" on the cover. Mark had no idea what that meant and was quite enthused about finding something that he had never heard of before. On the inside cover was an inscription that read, "To Luke, from Grandma."

Mark found Catherine and showed her the discovery. She also had never heard of such a book. "Why, this is incredible," she said. "It appears to be broken up into sixty-six individual sections with what appear to be everything from history to letters."

After a few more minutes, Catherine said, "Mark, what do you suppose we should do with this? Is this fact or fiction?"

"When was it printed?" They looked at the first few pages of the book and saw that the copyright date was 2012.

"Catherine, what do we know of that period in time?"

"Well, there was a nuclear arms race around then and many wars. I'd have to check the World Library archives to tell you more."

"Tell you what, how about if I call some of our friends and see what they know?" Mark placed a call on his Global Communication Device (GCD) and talked to his friends and associates at the World Science Foundation (WSF), which Mark was heading up that year. He sent a picture of the cover of the strange book along with the table of contents. None of his friends had ever heard of such a book either. All of them considered it to be an amazing find and worthy of much study.

Mark wanted to stay above board on any discovery he made, so he also contacted the World Police Force (WPF)—an agency that had been formed hundreds of years earlier as an outgrowth of a group that called itself NMR, or No More Religion. The officer called back within a few minutes and indicated that all was clear. Of course, no one at the WPF had any knowledge of the Bible at that time, because several hundred years earlier NMR had successfully destroyed all religious artifacts and there was no longer anyone alive who remembered anything about religion. The Record Destruct Dates (RDD) on these items had been about fifty years earlier (records were only kept for one hundred years on these sorts of artifacts). Thus, without realizing it, the WPF cleared the way for Mark to begin in-depth research on the find.

The next morning, Mark contacted the WSF to begin to form a research committee that would study the book. "Catherine, this is incredible," he later said to his wife. "Every member of the WSF from all around the world wants to be part of the research team. I've never had such a response from them. They're either bored or think there's something very peculiar about this discovery that's worth pursuing. I can't take them all. How do I limit the team?"

Catherine looked at him with a smile and said, "If this is the biggest problem you have with this endeavor, you'll be quite fortunate."

Chapter 16

Quest for the Truth

Mark had the book scanned and transmitted to each of the members of the WSF research committee. Each member was to read the entire book and then decipher and provide in-depth findings on one or more sections. What made their job a little easier was that this particular Bible happened to be a Study Bible and had many cross-references, study notes, maps and timelines. The main WSF computer database was to be the storage device for all the researchers' findings.

"This is absolutely fascinating," said Mark over the GCD to all the WSF members who had conferenced in. "This appears to be a historical account of a group of people. What I don't know is whether this account is supposed to be of people from Earth or from some other world. It seems that if it were of people from Earth, we'd surely have known about it before now. It's not like this could have been kept secret for the last 500 to 600 years."

"But it contradicts everything that we have been taught about the history of the human race or how the earth was created," replied Tom over the GCD. "All the information we have indicates that we evolved from lower-order life forms and that there was a sudden cataclysm that formed the galaxies and planets."

"And the timeline indicates that the birth of this Jesus person is the reason why time started to be counted in ascending order," said Alfred. "We had always been taught that this was due to the famous Roman census of Caesar Augustus, with B.C. being "Before Caesar" and A.C. being "After Caesar." But if you look at the timeline itself, it shows that B.C. was for "Before Christ" and A.D. was for "*Anno Domini*." The study notes indicate that *Anno Domini* is a Latin word meaning, "In the Year of Our Lord." (The term "A.D." had been changed to "A.C." during the persecution of the world religions that began around 2050 and lasted about 350 years.)

"The time has come for all of us at the WSF to start doing background checks on the history that we have been taught," said Mark. "We need to look for any gaps or possible tainting of our history books. I want you to all find whatever you can and report back in forty-eight hours. I'm sure that you all realize the importance of this. This could very well impact our way of life." All the members of the WSF agreed to get back together via GCD in forty-eight hours.

Mark spent the next few hours multiplexing between conducting historical research and reading the book he had found. At the appointed time, Mark contacted all the WSF on the GCD.

"OK, friends, what have you found?"

"All of the history books in the libraries I checked online were written within the last one hundred years," replied Alfred. "I found none before that date. That seems a bit fishy to me."

"I'm inclined to agree with you," replied Mark. Many of the other WSF members on the conference call agreed as well.

"I checked with the WPF and they allowed me to run a full check on their main security computers," said Tom. "There was a major set of records—I'd say more than several million—that were due for destruction about fifty years ago. There are no records as to what they were, but it is my belief that something happened that the WPF wanted to eliminate all trace of. What we need to figure out is what the WPF eliminated, and why. You know, guys, unless you format the storage area, data is not really deleted; only the path to it is removed. What do you think about my checking into undoing some of the deletion of the library and WPF records that could have been dated prior to fifty years ago?"

"I don't want to discourage you," said Mark, "but fifty years is a long time ago. I expect that the files have been defragmented by this time and there is nothing left to look at. If you want to see what you can find, I see nothing wrong with trying. What have the rest of you found?"

"On a hunch, I attempted to verify the linearity of carbon dating," said John. "What I found was that the dating was not really linear when you go back more than about 5,000 years. It would take a little explaining to go through my calculations, but suffice it to say that I am questioning the evolutionary dates."

"I took a look at the records of some of the fossils that were supposed to prove the evolutionary links between apes and humans," said Mitchell. "I found numerous weak links and also a few that looked as if they had been deliberately falsified. It will take me take a few more days to run a full verification, but I believe I'm correct."

"I decided to visit some cemeteries," said Hubert, "and I found that the inscription on some of the stones that were supposed to be more than 200 years old appeared to have been made more recently. To put it more bluntly, a carved gravestone for someone who died around 1600 should have looked as if it were from that period, not 200 years old. Good thing our methods of verification have improved during the last hundred years."

"Based on all of this new information, I don't believe we need to run any more checks," said Mark. "I think we have begun to realize that someone went to a lot trouble to obliterate some information. If our guess is correct and this book has some of the missing information, we need to find a way to verify the authority of the data contained in the book."

There was a long silence while each member of the team thought about a way to confirm the book. Eventually, Mark spoke up.

"Collectively, the members of the WSF are the most intelligent beings the world has ever produced. If there is a way to get this book authenticated, we should be able to find it. Remember what the definition of science is? Science is supposed to be able to prove facts through experimentation and repeatability. In other words, if this is history, why can't we repeat it?"

"Are you trying to say we should recreate the events ourselves?" asked Mitchell.

"Not exactly. The only way to really verify the events is to witness them for ourselves."

"You mean time travel?" asked Hubert.

"Exactly! It will be our intent to create a device that will allow us to travel back in time to view events, but not change them."

"Sort of like 'read only mode' on a computer storage device," said Tom.

"That's right. We will create a device that will allow us to go back in time to see the events that verify the book. We just need to go as observers. Regardless of how much we may feel the urge to help the people of the time period, we must resist. Of course, the only way to make sure that we do not interfere is to make it impossible to interact with the people of that time. After all, to change history would be catastrophic—we could affect our own existence or, worse, create a paradox in which existence itself would be jeopardized."

They all thought about what Mark said for a couple of minutes. Then, one by one, each of the members of the WSF agreed that this would be the best plan. After a few more minutes, they were thoroughly excited and couldn't wait for the project to start. They were acting more like children would who were trying to guess what would happen on their birthday.

"One more thing," said Mark. "Under no circumstances should we design this machine with the ability to go forward in time—that is, from the time in which we came."

"Wise idea, Mark," said John. "We don't want anyone to try and know the future and then use that information to gain some financial advantage—or even to know the circumstances of their own death."

"You obviously got my point," said Mark. "In any case, we'll need to divide up the work. Catherine will study the book to figure out what would be the best times and places to travel back to once we get the device ready."

Mark divided up the team into separate groups and had each group work in the specific regions in the world that had previously been known as "continents." The team responsible for region 1 (formerly Europe) was to work on the time calculator and keeper, which included the time limiter called a "governor." This particular piece of software would guarantee that the members of the research teams could not travel beyond the point they started from or go back to a time before there was a physical world with breathable air. Although this task seemed easy enough at first glance, the researchers knew that reading all the sensors and computing an accurate time was going to be quite a challenge.

The team in charge of region 2 (formerly Asia) was to work on the problem of making sure that none of the team members would be seen by the inhabitants of the time periods they were visiting. This, too, was not an easy task, as this was not to be a view portal but a live transport in which the WSF would be physically in the other world. In addition, they needed to make sure that they would not change the past or accidentally bump into anyone and cause a problem in the timeline—or inadvertently get themselves killed.

The team for region 3 (formerly Africa) was to work on the problem of creating a Universal Translator (UT). They needed this device because the teams had no way of understanding Aramaic, Hebrew or even old Greek. They really didn't know what type of language the people they would be visiting would speak.

The team for region 4 (formerly North America) would work on the problem of disassembling molecules for transport. In other words, they would try to figure out how to convert the people traveling back in time into a form that would make it easy to move them from one time to another while keeping them safe from harm. Everything was to be automatic in order to make sure that there would be no human interaction and so as to cut down on mistakes. Naturally, the team also had the job of reassembling the people once they were finished being transported.

The team responsible for region 5 (formerly South America) in conjunction with the team for region 6 (formerly Australia) had the job of finding the best method of transport. They were to come up with several options and eventually choose the best one. The one thing that the team members soon agreed on was that all real-time machines would require spatial movement, for otherwise the machine would collide with itself as it attempted to go back in time and create a paradox.

This meant that the teams really did have to divide up the work once again. The team for region 5 would work on the transport mechanism, while the team for region 6 would have to work on the vehicle. The vehicle did not need as much physical space to carry people, as they would be disassembled in transport. Thus there would not be a space problem, even though region 4 was to account for about one hundred people, just to be safe. The vehicle also needed to be able to travel faster than light speed.

The transport mechanism was essentially a piece of software that controlled the whole process. It would need to interface with the vehicle sensors, control the path and speed of the vehicle, automatically bring the vehicle to the right location, know when to disassemble the participants and when to reassemble them, interface with the time computer software that the team for region 1 was to create, and interface with the software that the region 2 team was developing for when they arrived at the destination so that no one could see them on arrival.

Since Catherine would be doing the majority of the planning for where the teams would travel, and since Mark was conveniently married to her, the two had plenty of time to talk things over.

"Mark," said Catherine. "As I've been reading the book, I've come to some very interesting conclusions."

"OK, dear. Let's hear them."

"First, the entire book seems to point to or revolve around a particular person named 'Jesus.' Thus, our initial time destination should be related to His presence in history."

"That sounds quite logical."

"Next, I believe that our initial target point in history should be at the time of the birth of Jesus. Specifically, we should follow the shepherds from just before the angels visited them to the place of Jesus' birth."

"Again, I see no fault in your logic."

"I believe that the second point in history that we should target is during the last week or so of Jesus' life on Earth, right before He died. This time period should include what the book indicates is the raising of Lazarus from the dead, the Last Supper, His time spent in the Garden of Gethsemane, His death and His resurrection."

"You haven't said anything I'd disagree with yet."

"If we are convinced about the truth of the book at that point, we should take a very close look at Jesus' life and teachings. After that, we can talk about visiting other times and people within the book. If the events are as the book describes, it will revolutionize history and our way of life for all time. I would highly recommend that we be prepared for this."

"You bring up some very good points. Let me talk to the rest of the WSF—and maybe even the WPF—to see if they have any recommendations on what we should do if all this turns out to be true."

Catherine took a deep breath. "Truthfully, I'm having trouble figuring out exactly what date some of these events took place. From the study notes I can get to the year, but not to any more specific timeframe. I'll see if I can narrow it down some more."

"If you get stuck, I think Justin might be able to help out. He's always been quite good at history. Give him a call and at least prepare him for what may come his way."

"OK, love."

Although it appeared at first that the team from region 6 would have the toughest job, their task actually didn't take them that long to complete. This was because scientists in the WSF had already conducted research on developing a spacecraft that would travel faster than light. However, for this experiment, the craft would have to go faster than light in an orbit around the Earth in one direction in order to get to the past and go the opposite direction to get back to the future. This would require some extreme modifications to allow for the vast amounts of heat that would be generated on the spacecraft due to the great speeds it would travel in an orbit. The craft would have to go more than seven revolutions around the Earth per second in order to get near the speed of light.

In a short time, Mark received a call from Matthew from region 4. "Mark, we've completed basic testing and are ready for a live test."

The next day, many people gathered to watch the first live trial. All of the members of the region 4 group were in attendance, as were some of the main WSF leaders.

"All right, everyone," said Mark. "We've conducted several successful tests with a guinea pig. Who would like to be our first human guinea pig?"

"I'll do it!" replied Matthew without hesitation.

Mark set the controls for the trial as Matthew came forward.

"OK, Matthew," said Mark. "Stand over there on that platform on the spot marked with an 'X.' Let's set the countdown at ten. Ten, nine, eight, seven, six, five, four, three, two, one…Energize!"

Mark pushed the dematerialize button. Instantly, Matthew disappeared.

"Well," said Mark, "it looks as if the first half of the experiment worked. Now we need to verify that Matthew's molecules are safe in storage and then bring him back."

Some of the other scientists did some quick checks and managed to verify that Matthew was safe. It was now time to bring him back. Mark selected the materialize button, but instantly there was an explosion that destroyed the machine and injured several of the WSF members that were standing nearby.

"Is everyone OK?" asked Mark. "I think we may have lost Matthew."

Although some of the people were hurt, they were only superficial wounds. All present mourned for Matthew and wondered if there was anything they could have done to prevent the accident.

The teams all got back together the next day and started to theorize what had happened. On close examination and some reworking of the math, they realized that a calculated constant for one of their components had been off by an order of magnitude. This problem had only occurred because they had done the experiment on the guinea pig only minutes before the live test and the equipment didn't have an adequate chance to cool back down. With a larger component, this would not have occurred.

All of the WSF members realized that they had been working at a grueling pace. As a result, they decided that it would be wise to slow down a little and verify all the computations before again stating that they were ready to go.

Nine long months passed. At last, the teams declared victory and were finally ready to go.

Chapter 17

Time to Go Back

"Today," began Mark, "we are at the most important point in our known history. We have the ability to go back in time and see whether everything we have been taught is true or false. We need to be prepared to accept the fact that the history of the world as we have known it may have been manufactured. Are you all ready to accept this possibility?"

"We are!" said the group in unison.

"OK, then. Catherine, please set our destination and time, and then all of us will go on to the platform."

"Ready?" said Catherine once all of the members had gathered on the platform. "Commencing transport." With that, she pushed the button to start the sequence of events that would get them back in time. First, all the people dematerialized and were stored on the ship. Next, the ship powered up, ran a self-test and then took off. The craft accelerated to near light speed and went in an orbit around the Earth. As it did so, time slowed down and then started going backward.

When the teams approached the time coordinate that Catherine had programmed, the ship entered a standard orbit and then followed a flight plan that would take it toward the Middle East. The ship actually set down in an area outside Bethlehem, but within visual sight of it. Because the ship was invisible, the occupants did not have to worry about being seen.

Soon, the occupants were reassembled and stood outside the spacecraft, completely in awe of what they just experienced. The time that they had arrived was about the third hour of the day, which we know as nine A.M. They saw people in caravans walking to and fro, carrying large sacks of grain and fine linen. The people looked rather odd to the WSF members, as they had never seen people in clothes such as those worn by these people.

Mark decided to speak up first. "Based on the time of day, I'd say that we made a slight error in our calculations. If we can get close to some of these people, we might be able to find out something. Turn on your translators and follow a few people into town to see if you can get some information."

The WSF team members began to follow some of the caravans into town. For the size of the town, there were a lot of people. Just then, Catherine remembered something.

"Mark, these people are here for the census. We've come to the right time period—we just need to find the right stable and the right shepherds."

Mark picked up his GCD. "OK, everyone spread out. We're looking for shepherds in the outlying fields, a man and his wife who would be ready to have a baby at any time now, and a stable."

The task ended up being far more complicated than everyone initially thought. There were people everywhere. Because a census was taking place, some of the WSF thought that it would be best to stand by the places people registered for the census. Other members searched out what they thought were local inns. Others did a whole lot of walking and went to the outlying areas, looking for the shepherds.

"Mark?" said Catherine.

"Yes, dear?"

"Since it's morning and I don't think we missed the time of Jesus' birth, I believe that Mary and Joseph would not yet have arrived. I believe that our group should split up and begin to mingle with these people and record conversations so that the UT can learn about the language."

"You realize that there's more than one language being spoken here, right?"

"I'm aware of that, but I still think that the UT should be able to put together a pretty good word bank regardless of how many languages there are."

Mark was not only surprised but also ecstatic to see how quickly the UT picked up the languages. He went over to one of the census-taker tables and listened as people spoke and the UT translated. Although the people's words were a little broken at first, it took less than an hour before Mark could understand complete conversations.

One older man with a long beard was saying to the census-taker, "All you're doing is figuring out who we are in order to tax us. We're already taxed heavily. Why don't you take our cloaks as well?"

One of the Roman soldiers guarding the census-taker responded in a very harsh tone. "Any more comments like that and I'll take your cloak, your staff and your entire purse as well."

The man gave the soldier a glare and replied, "When the Messiah comes, he will overthrow all of you."

"Quiet down, dog," replied the Roman soldier. "Your Messiah hasn't come for thousands of years. What makes you think that he will show up any time soon?"

"God has never failed us. We have failed Him, but He has never failed us." As the man walked away, he spoke some other words that Mark could not hear. The UT was unable to pick up the voice with all the other people in the area.

Mark was quite pleased. He had actually heard a real person talk about a Messiah, just as the book indicated. He used his communicator to spread the news. "I've got some good news for you all. One of the people who came in for the census talked about the coming of the Messiah. Catherine heard it as well. By the way, my compliments to the UT development team. This is a real fine piece of work."

Mark and Catherine could hear some responses over the communicator—"Thanks, boss" seemed to be the gist of it. All the WSF members were quite excited that they at least seemed to have landed in the right area.

As the day wore on, the group members learned other facts. People talked of father Abraham and Isaac and Jacob. They talked of David, Solomon's Temple, Moses and even Adam and Eve. All of these were people that were mentioned in the book.

"Mark?" said Catherine.

"Yes, my love?"

"You realize that we're getting a lot of confirmation of the people and places that the book described."

"I've been thinking of that. We already know that history as we know it has been drastically altered for some unknown reason. We may or may not find out what that is on this trip, though I expect that we'll figure it out within a year."

"You're likely correct. I'm just hoping that it won't take a whole year."

By late afternoon, many people were looking for lodging for the night. Catherine noticed a man walking a donkey that was carrying a woman who looked very pregnant. The girl seemed quite young; Catherine estimated that she couldn't have been more than fifteen years old. It was obvious the journey was tiring for her. Catherine was very sympathetic and wanted to act like a mother, but she knew that there was nothing to be done, as they had made it impossible to interfere.

Catherine followed the man as he went to be registered and then, when he was turned away, as he started looking for a place to spend the night. She sent word to Mark and the others that she had likely found Mary and Joseph. Some of the WSF members came with Mark and Catherine to follow Mary and Joseph.

Joseph stopped one man to talk. "My wife is about to have a baby," he said. "Is there any place we can stay for the night?"

The man looked at Mary and shook his head. "Bethlehem is not a big place. It's nothing like Jerusalem. The only place I can think of that might have room is a small inn at the south side of town. An older couple run it, and they always seem to come up with some place for people to stay."

"Well, that's the best lead I've had so far. Thank you for your trouble."

The man and his wife went to the south side of town and found the small inn. There was a small cave about one hundred yards in the back of it in which several animals were housed. The man spoke kindly to his wife and said, "Mary, I'll go in and see what I can find."

"Hurry, Joseph," replied the pregnant girl. "I've been having contractions all day. I sure wish my mother or my cousin Elizabeth was with me right now."

Catherine badly wanted to help; it just tore her up to have to stand by and do nothing. But all she could do is watch as Joseph went inside the inn and spoke to the innkeeper. He came out a few minutes later and went to speak to Mary.

"Mary, the best the innkeeper had to offer us was the little cave in the back. I'm sorry."

"Right now, I don't care what the place looks like. I just need to get down from this donkey and lie down until the baby comes."

A few minutes later the couple arrived at the cave. Joseph helped Mary down from the donkey and gave her a hug.

"It'll take me a little while to get this area prepared for you. With the grace of God, I'll have it nice and comfortable in no time."

In a surprisingly short amount of time, Joseph managed to move the animals outside and prepare the cave for Mary. The manger was made out of rock, just like all the rest found in that area. Joseph removed all the manure and laid some fresh straw on the ground and in the manger. He also placed some straw in a big pile to one side of the cave for Mary to lie on and possibly have the baby. He also laid some blankets on the ground to make it a little warmer for Mary. Although Mary was an incredible girl, she was still a teenager in labor.

"OK, Mary, it's time to come lie down and rest."

Mary looked at Joseph and with a grateful sigh said, "Praise the Lord!"

It was getting dark and the WSF members assigned to find the shepherds couldn't figure out which ones were going to be visited by the angels. Eventually the members split up and each set of five followed a group of shepherds. The WSF teams didn't quite prepare for the weather, however. The night was cool, and they hadn't brought any warm clothes. So they decided to stand close to the fires that the shepherds were building. The warmth spread over them, which made the waiting much more tolerable.

Mark and Catherine still wished they could help Mary and Joseph, but they knew that was out of the question. They were there to observe and not to interfere in history. As the night passed, it was obvious to Mark and Catherine that Mary's contractions were getting closer together and much stronger. Joseph held Mary's hand and let her head rest on him as much as he could. He had seen many animals being born but never humans, as this was forbidden in their society. Mary had only seen a few babies being born, but she had never taken part in the procedure herself. She usually ran errands for the adults and the midwife.

"Mary, is there anything I can get for you?" Joseph said to his wife.

Mary shook her head no. Joseph dampened a towel and placed it on her forehead. When she smiled, Joseph knew that he had done the right thing.

Soon, everyone could see Mary grunting as if she were pushing. Joseph moved her clothing in such a way that the baby would have an easy passage. With only a few pushes, the baby was out. There was a lot of crying by Mary, Joseph and the baby—not to mention by the twenty or so other witnesses from the WSF.

The baby was immediately placed on Mary's stomach and allowed to nurse. Joseph made some strips of cloth out of some of the old tunics that he had brought and wrapped the baby in them.

"Catherine, I don't remember any of your births being that easy," said Mark.

"Believe me, they weren't."

Mark looked at the other attendees. "What do the rest of you think?"

None of them had ever witnessed a birth like this before. All of them considered themselves quite fortunate to have been there.

The WSF members that had remained in the fields with the groups of shepherds were getting pretty disheartened, as they still couldn't figure out which shepherds were going to be the ones visited by the angels.

"Martin, do you ever think that we'll find the right shepherds?" asked Bridget.

"I don't really know. You'd think with all the amazing science we know that we'd have calculated a better time or place."

About fifty feet from where they were standing, a group of shepherds were warming themselves by a fire. All of a sudden there was a bright flash of light, and then something that resembled a superbeing spoke. "Do not be afraid. I have come to bring you good news. Unto you is born this day in the city of David a Savior, which is Christ the Lord. Let this be a sign unto you. You shall find a baby wrapped in strips of cloth and lying in a manger."

Immediately the sky was filled with beings like the one who spoke. They sang and gave glory to God. Then, just as impressively as they had come, they were gone.

The shepherds said to one another, "Come, let us go see this thing that the Lord has made known unto us."

Martin and Bridget were thrilled. They had never seen anything this incredible in their lives. Fortunately, they had made a digital recording of the event.

"Come on, Bridget," said Martin. "Let's go follow the shepherds. Eventually they'll show up at the stable."

"Right with you there, guy."

Martin decided to let the others know what had happened and that he had recorded it. All were happy at the news. Martin also let the other people in the fields know the news so that they wouldn't have to keep standing out in the cold waiting for something to happen.

Once the events of the night were over and daylight had dawned on the horizon, the little WSF group gathered together. Mark spoke up and said, "We have seen and recorded events that modern man has never seen before. The angels that spoke to those shepherds were not only real but also confirm the events that were written in the book. We should now decide what events we would like to see next in history. This has been truly remarkable, wouldn't you say everyone?"

The WSF members wholeheartedly agreed and came to the decision that the next events they should witness were those surrounding the resurrection of Jesus. They chose this time because it was not only a supernatural event but also one that was the turning point in history for much of mankind for thousands of years.

"OK everybody, back to the ship," said Mark. "Looks like it's time for a leap into the future about thirty-three years."

Chapter 18

A Change in Plans

The WSF transport ship landed a little bit north of where it left, just outside the city of Jerusalem. From the looks of the people around the city, it was quite obvious that it was the Sabbath. People were doing no work, and many were just talking among themselves. The Roman soldiers were attempting to keep the peace and were carefully watching everyone.

One soldier said to another, "We need to watch out for any rebellion or other such ruckus. Those followers of that false king of the Jews may do anything. Let's go check out that tomb where they buried him just to see if everything is stable."

"Sure thing. I don't really know where they stuck him, so you lead the way."

Mark turned to the others and said, "Although it would have been better if we had arrived a little earlier in the week, this is a great break for us. We'll follow these two soldiers and just wait until tomorrow morning, when the action starts."

All the WSF members agreed and decided to follow the soldiers directly to the tomb. It was about a thirty-minute walk before they arrived.

"Hey Mark," said Harold. "I've had more exercise on this trip than I've had in years. These local people are extremely fit. Even the older ones are in better shape than I am."

"I have a feeling that all of us are in agreement with you, my friend. Now I know why Mary didn't have that much trouble with the birth."

The soldiers walked on ahead and had a short chat with the two guards that were posted on either side of the tomb. Once they were satisfied that everything was in order, they left the area.

"What do you say we do an internal scan to verify there's still a body in there?" said Mark. "We don't want to wait until morning for nothing."

"Excellent idea," they all said in unison.

"Martin, do you have that scanner that I asked you to bring?"

"Got it right here, Mark."

"OK, aim it at entrance to the tomb and see what you find."

Martin picked up the scanner, which was only about the size of a cell phone, programmed it to look for human remains and then calibrated it to enable it to penetrate solid rock. He aimed the scanner at the tomb, and within a minute he had the results.

"It looks like the remains of a body. The person is a male between thirty to thirty-five years of age and has been dead about twenty-four hours. According to the readings, the body is pretty mangled."

"Can you tell how he died?" asked Mark.

"From the look of it, he was tortured. There is a good-sized hole in each wrist and each foot. There's a big puncture wound in his side and numerous abrasions on his back. My guess is that he died from blood loss, but we would have to perform a slightly better analysis to be sure. Of course, you can't do that from outside solid rock."

Mark looked at the group and said, "Looks like we're in the right place at the right time. Now all we have to do is wait until morning. You can each go look around Jerusalem and record anything interesting that you find for historical purposes. Meet back here at eleven P.M. tonight. It may be a long night, but we don't want to miss anything important. I expect that nothing will happen until we get close to sunrise."

"This will probably be our last stop," said Catherine, "and we'll be going back home by noon tomorrow. So…go ahead and look around as much as you want today."

With that, the group scattered. Mark and Catherine went into Jerusalem and looked at the Temple. It was a marvelous structure. They noticed that although there were no animal sacrifices taking place due to the Sabbath, there were still a number of people going to worship—and the moneychangers and tax collectors were also quite abundant.

Catherine looked around. "Mark, think of the workmanship involved in making the Temple and the surroundings. They must have had thousands of slaves working for years to complete this structure."

"And there was no machinery to move any of this. It was all built by manual labor."

Martin and Bridget were both around thirty years of age. They always tried to find excuses to be near each other, and this seemed to be an opportune time. They decided to see if they could find the Mount of Olives that they had read about in "The Book." After a short discussion, they tramped off in a direction that they thought would give them the greatest chance of success.

Martin was really in love with Bridget, and as they walked together he was getting a little tongue-tied. She could tell that he was having a little trouble with conversation when he said, "This really is a most fascinating trip."

She looked at him and laughed. "You never talk like that, Martin. What's on your mind?" The two were approaching a grove of olive trees that seemed to be a really romantic spot.

"Wow! What a neat spot," said Martin, snapping out of his awkwardness.

"I've got to agree with you there, buddy."

Martin turned and faced Bridget, who was just a few inches shorter than he. As they looked at each other, he reached out to take her hand. She shook her head from side to side. Martin was taken aback and felt a little foolish, believing that he must have been a little too forward.

"No, you fool," said Bridget, smiling. "I want a real hug." With that, she opened up her arms and held him tight. She looked up into his eyes and after a couple of seconds they kissed as though they had been on a trip and had not seen each other in weeks. After a few minutes, they were still holding each other tightly. Finally, Martin spoke up and said, "I love you Bridget."

"I love you too, Martin."

"Will you marry me when we get back home?"

Bridget looked at him for a few seconds, smiled and kissed him.

"I'm taking that as a yes," said Martin.

"I would if I were you!"

The city gates were about to close for the night, so all the WSF members who were in the city left and reassembled out by the tomb. The only two that were missing were Martin and Bridget.

"Where are those two?" asked Mark.

"If I had to guess, I'd say they wanted some time alone together," replied Catherine.

"What do you mean?"

"Oh, Mark. It does seem to take a woman to notice these things. They seem to have quite a thing for each other."

"I hadn't really noticed."

"My point exactly."

Within a few minutes, Martin and Bridget came walking up, hand in hand. Catherine looked at Mark and said, "Now do you believe me?"

Mark looked at her and smiled. "That's why I married you. You're definitely the more observant of the two of us."

It was midnight by that point and the whole WSF assembled at the tomb. Mark directed each of them to be stationed at different places so that they could witness the resurrection from different angles and record the event. The members of the group were far too nervous to go to sleep, so even after a number of hours had passed they were all still awake and alert.

The sun was just about to rise and the guards at the tomb were yawning. They had just begun to discuss when their relief would arrive when a flash of light brighter than anything any of them had ever seen before shone around the tomb. Suddenly, an angel appeared and rolled the stone away as though it weighed only a few pounds.

When the guards saw what was taking place, they fell face down as though they were dead. Mark grabbed one of the scanners to see what was inside the tomb. To his surprise, he found that there was nothing there. The body was gone. "What am I thinking?" Mark said to himself. "This is exactly what we came here to figure out. It happened just as we were hoping."

After the angel left, the two guards stood up, looked at each other and ran away.

"Based on the recorded events in the book, I don't think we'll have to wait very long for the women to show up and for Jesus to appear to them," said Catherine.

"We already have enough data to confirm what the book has stated," said Mark. "After Jesus appears to them, our work here is complete and we can go home."

After about an hour, the WSF crew saw a couple of women coming up the path to the tomb. "OK, everyone," said Mark. "Pay attention. Check to see that all your recording devices are on and that we are positioned at various locations to get the best viewing angles and audio recordings."

The women reached the tomb and saw that the stone had been rolled away and that there were no guards. They went into the tomb to look for Jesus' body, but it was gone. Immediately, the entire WSF group saw a figure dressed in white garments appear from out of nowhere. A light shone around the man. At first the WSF team members could not identify a source for the light, but they finally deduced that the light was coming from the man himself. The women, now coming out of the tomb, saw the man and mistook him for the gardener.

"Excuse me sir," one of the women said, "but someone has taken my Lord and I don't know where they have put him. Do you know where they have placed him so that we can go attend to the body?"

The man looked at her and said, "Mary."

Instantly the women recognized him and yelled out, "Raboni!"

The man looked at the women with a smile and said, "Go and tell my brothers that I have risen just as I had said and that I will see them soon."

The man vanished from their sight and the women excitedly ran from the tomb back the way they had come.

Mark looked at the group and declared, "I think we've accomplished our mission here. The events of the book are real. Although this is good data, I'm not sure what our next step will be once we get back home."

When he had completed his statement, a flash suddenly appeared near them. It was Jesus, and He was looking directly at Mark. He smiled and spoke in a warm and loving way.

"Children, come gather round."

The entire WSF group looked at each other and then at Mark. Mark gestured for everyone to do as Jesus had said. Although Jesus should not have been able to see them due to their advanced technology, it appeared that He was able to do so. "You have done well to come and learn," He said to the group. "Although the book you have found has everything you need to learn about the truth, you still will not fully understand. Come, let me touch each of you and fill you with the Holy Spirit so that you may proclaim the good news to the future generations from which you have come."

Although the WSF members were still not sure what to do, they seemed to be drawn to this man. Mark and

Catherine went up first. Jesus put His hands on them, and instantly they felt more relaxed than they had ever been in their lives. They felt a strength flow through them unlike any they had ever felt before.

"You have believed because you have seen. For you, this was the only way you could know the truth. Blessed are they who will believe on your words."

Each of the other members of the group went up to Jesus, and He touched them as well. Martin and Bridget came up together. Jesus looked at them and smiled. He whispered something to them and they were awestruck. After Jesus had finished talking to them, they held each other's hands and went back to where they had previously stood, hugging each other tighter than they had ever done before. We will never know what Jesus said to them, but we can guess that it had to do with their lives in the future.

Jesus turned His attention back to the entire crowd. "You are to be my disciples in the future generation," He said. "It was I who placed the idea in a little boy's mind many years in the future to bury a book that would eventually be found by a man who had a quest for the truth. I know that you have many questions as to why the events of your past led to what appeared to be the total elimination of religion. These questions will be answered when we meet again at the end of the world. The book will be your guide, but remember that I will always be with you in spirit. The Spirit of the Lord is now upon each of you, and you will be able to perform feats that you never thought possible so that others may be drawn to the truth. Goodbye for now."

With that, Jesus vanished from their sight.

The group remained speechless for a few minutes. This Jesus was obviously not bound by time and could move about freely in whatever dimension He chose. Each of them had been a believer for only a few minutes, and though they still did not comprehend everything, they knew that Jesus was God and that a hole in their lives had been filled.

Mark spoke up and addressed the group. "I realize that we are all thinking that this is like a dream and that we are all wondering if it can really be true. I assure you that all we have witnessed has been quite real and that we are now part of a major plan to evangelize the future generations. Let's gather all of our equipment. We have a lot of work to do back home."

Martin and Bridget looked at each other. Bridget put her arms around Martin's neck and with a loving smile whispered into his ear, "More than he knows."

Pleasant
Word

To order additional copies of this title call:
1-877-421-READ (7323)
or please visit our web site at
www.pleasantwordbooks.com

If you enjoyed this quality custom published book,
drop by our web site for more books and information.

www.winepressgroup.com
"Your partner in custom publishing."

Printed in the United States
109083LV00001B/20/A